Religion in Overalls

Religion in Overalls

By
William G. Johnsson

Southern Publishing Association, Nashville, Tennessee

This book was
Edited by Richard Coffen
Designed by Dean Tucker
and Mark O'Connor
Cover design by Bob Redden

Type set: 11/12 Century Schoolbook

Printed in U.S.A.

Library of Congress Cataloging in Publication Data

Johnsson, William G   1934-
    Religion in overalls.

    1. Bible. N.T. Matthew—Criticism, interpretation, etc.
I. Title.
BS2575.2.J64   225'.2'06   77-22464
ISBN 0-8127-0143-7

Dedication

For Noelene
Without whom not

Contents

Preface

Religion in Overalls springs from two concerns.

First, I have felt increasingly troubled by the widening gulf between ivory tower and pew. An enormous amount of scholarly study has focused on the Bible in recent years, but most of it remains the province of the elite—those who understand Greek, Hebrew, German, French, and the jargon of the discipline. Yet much of this study can directly or indirectly benefit the minister and thinking layman.

It seems to me that the very nature of Biblical studies calls for an effort to make the fruits of scholarly research available to the layman. Otherwise, the study of the Bible may eventually become no more than a study in antiquities. This, then, is the initial concern of *Religion in Overalls*: to present some of the results of current Biblical studies.

Second, over several years the conviction has grown that Matthew's Gospel has a message of unusual significance for the church today, and I think we continue to bypass it only at the church's peril. The first Gospel has something to say which will keep the church on balance in these changing and surprising times.

I have in mind particularly the so-called Jesus Movement and the return to charismatic Christianity during the past decade. I do not intend to review these developments. Already the literature which seeks to plot their contours and to evaluate them is considerable. Rather, I propose that we take a close look at Matthew's Gospel *against this background*. I think we shall find that the message of the first Gospel is strikingly appropriate and needful to Christian life today.

I claim no great originality for this work but have drawn freely on the labors of New Testament scholars from various countries, especially as they relate to the Book of Matthew. I owe a particular debt to the work of the German scholars Bornkamm, Barth, and Held, whose studies of Matthew in recent years have opened up new vistas.

Yet the sifting of the mass of Biblical data from the scholars is my own. The thematic approach adopted likewise bears my own stamp, which will be obvious to other New Testament scholars.

Here I wish to give acknowledgment to the fertile mind of Professor Leander E. Keck. During one of his seminars at Vanderbilt University several years ago, the relevance of Matthew to the church today was first suggested to me. Reflection on that seed thought eventually led to the development of this book. I should like also to acknowledge the contribution of John R. Jones, who critically read the manuscript and provided several helpful suggestions.

A final word. Since this is primarily a book for ministers and laymen, I have not burdened it down with a load of scholarly paraphernalia and have tried to avoid scholarly jargonese, making the notes as simple as possible. Further, the approach has been to keep the text moving and keep it Bible-centered. Supporting material of a secondary character appears in the notes.

Serious Bible study is exciting. I find Matthew to be an absorbing book, and it is with the hope that many fellow Christians may experience the thrill of new insights that I have prepared this work. Thus, while *Religion in Overalls* may not come under the usual category of entertaining, I think it may interest the one who takes the Bible seriously.

William G. Johnsson
Andrews University
Berrien Springs, Michigan

Chapter 1

Looking at Matthew's Gospel

Every Christian knows that the Gospel of Matthew is the first document in the New Testament. But how many have ever pondered the question as to why this should be so?

Our New Testament is familiar to us as a collection of twenty-seven works, and we tend to think that these writings always existed in this combination, or did so almost immediately from their inception. But when we look at the young church of the first three centuries, we have to change our perspective: Our well-known documents were circulating individually, not in combination. And there were many other Christian writings in the stream—gospels like the Gospel of Thomas or the Gospel of Peter; rivals to our Acts of the Apostles such as the Acts of Paul and Thecla; other letters such as First and Second Clement; even another book like our Revelation: the Shepherd of Hermas, highly regarded in certain areas of the church.[1]

---

[1] The list of writings is much longer than this. These are only sample illustrations. We should note, however, that these non-canonical writings at no time enjoyed *universal* support. Some, however, were very popular in particular places; e.g., both Clement of Alexandria and Origen viewed the author of 1 Clement as the Clement mentioned in Philippians 4:3, and the author of the Shepherd of Hermas as the Hermas of Romans 16:14. Irenaeus certainly regarded the Shepherd as Scripture.

A consensus gradually emerged among Christians as to which writings should be counted as Scripture and which should be left out. We know that the question was settled by AD 367.[2] The history of the canon is a fascinating study—how some documents well thought of by certain churches eventually were excluded; how other "late starters," as it were, found a place; the factors and reasons which led to the eventual consensus—but it cannot detain us here. We come back to Matthew's Gospel. Why did the church give this work pride of place in the finished list?

The obvious answers quickly fall short. First of all, Matthew's Gospel is not the earliest of the New Testament writings. The books of the New Testament are not arranged in a chronological order. In fact, the oldest work among the twenty-seven is beyond question one of Paul's letters—probably his first epistle to the Thessalonian believers or his letter to the Galatians.[3]

Second, Matthew's is not the oldest of the Four Gospels. When we closely study Matthew, Mark, and Luke, we find amazing similarities— at times a word-for-word correspondence.[4] On the other hand we encounter drastic differences in the accounts, not only in the sayings of Jesus, but in the ordering of events and matters of fact.[5]

The tangled relationships of these three Gospels comprise the famous "synoptic problem" of Biblical studies. To try to sort them out is like working through a detective story—except that it is more interesting and profitable! A careful comparison of Matthew's, Mark's, and Luke's Gospels does point to one conclusion, however. Mark's is the oldest, because both Matthew and Luke draw upon his writings.[6] Almost all Protestant scholars are now convinced of this point, but Roman Catholic Bible students are more hesitant, since it conflicts with an official statement of their church.

---

[2] The Easter letter of Athanasius in that year lists as Scripture the twenty-seven documents which now form our New Testament.

[3] The Pauline epistles are not arranged in chronological order. The reader will notice that the order is basically decided by *length*. (Note that the authorship of Hebrews was disputed for several centuries; hence, although it was eventually ascribed to Paul, this document was placed last in the Pauline group.) As to which letter Paul wrote first, it is clear that 1 Thessalonians was written in the early 50's. The letter to the Galatians may have preceded it, however; the question turns on the precise identification of the Galatians.

[4] The reader of the Synoptic Gospels (i.e., Matthew, Mark, and Luke) will already be aware of this in a general way. The

We must look again to the early years of Christianity if we wish to discover the reason for the priority given to Matthew's Gospel. When we turn to the Christian writings of the second and third centuries and notice their use of the twenty-seven New Testament documents, we are immediately impressed by the concentration upon Matthew. Over and over there are references and quotations from this document— more than from any other of the writings which eventually became the canon.

So the picture at last is clear: The early church highly esteemed Matthew's Gospel and constantly used it for instruction and worship. Today if Protestants are asked which are the most significant portions of the New Testament, most will probably suggest Paul's letters. This is the heritage of the Reformation. We remember Luther at study in Wittenberg University, preparing his lectures on Romans and later on Galatians. (In those days there were no time limits on courses, which continued until the subject matter was fully covered. So his studies in Romans ran for more than a year!) As he struggled to understand the text, gradually the light dawned, and the greatest upheaval in the history of Christendom resulted. But in the early centuries of Christianity, Matthew's writing rather than Paul's gave direction to the church.

following parallel passages offer good examples: the healing of the paralytic (Mark 2:1-12; Matthew 9:1-8; Luke 5:17-26), the feeding of the 5,000 (Mark 6:32-44; Matthew 14:13-21; Luke 9:10-17), the rich man (Mark 10:23-31; Matthew 19:23-30; Luke 18:24-30), and Bartimaeus (Mark 10:46-52; Matthew 20:29-34; Luke 18:35-43). Numerous other parallels occur.

[5] Apart from the examples listed above, where differences as well as similarities exist, note particularly the rejection at Nazareth (Mark 6:1-6; Matthew 13:53-58; Luke 4:16-30) and the teaching of Jesus in Mark 13:9-13 and Matthew 10:17-22.

[6] While I consider this matter established, a few Protestant scholars continue to argue strongly against it. The argument for the priority of Mark rests principally on the *sequence* of the material in the Synoptic

Matthew and the Church Today

Of course Protestants do not wholly neglect Matthew. Simply because it ranks first among the Gospels, Christians often turn to it for retelling the story of Jesus. Most of all, however, Matthew alone relates the famous Sermon on the Mount. This account of Jesus' words finds its place in works of literature, selections from the world's religions, and even the public worship services of a Hindu such as Mahatma Gandhi.

But in general, Protestants have not given the weight to Matthew that Roman Catholics have. Indeed, some Protestants, taking Paul as the touchstone of the gospel, have gone so far as to accuse Matthew of a legalistic type of Christianity, of an ignorance of righteousness by faith. They would draw a sharp line between Paul and Matthew—and place themselves solidly on Paul's side. Catholics, on the other hand, have adhered more closely to the practice of the early centuries of Christianity in looking to Matthew as the preeminent Christian document. Their interest is not without dogmatic grounds: Only Matthew has the saying about Peter and the rock! (16:18).[7]

Perhaps Protestants should take a new look at Matthew. They will find there instruction which comes with peculiar force and appropriateness to the present situation of the church. We can better appreciate this possibility if we first consider the way in which the New Testament canon functions, then look around us to see the world in which the church finds itself today.

Gospels: The sequence of Matthew and Luke is never the same unless Mark agrees with them, and their sequence is always the same where Mark is in agreement.

[7] The verse immediately following contains the statement about "the keys of the kingdom of heaven."

The New Testament Canon

Our remarks concerning the supposed conflict between Paul and Matthew highlight a problem which worries many—the New Testament (and the Old Testament even more so) does not always seem consistent with itself. If God inspired each of the writings, it is argued, why should we encounter differences? The classic example is the apparent contradiction between Paul and James. Whereas Paul limits salvation to those who have faith without works, James declares that "a man is justified by works and not by faith alone" (James 2:24, RSV*).

We will find our way through the difficulty and be able to see how the Book of Matthew may speak with particular power to our age only if we take time to examine our concepts of inspiration, the nature of the New Testament documents, and the unity of the Scriptures.

-----

* All Bible quotations are taken from the Revised Standard Verson unless otherwise noted.

The Muslim believes that his holy book, the Koran, is an exact copy of a heavenly Koran. Every jot and tittle of the heavenly pattern was conveyed to the prophet Muhammad. Some Christians have a similar view of the Bible. They believe that God *dictated* the Sacred Canon word by word. But that idea of inspiration is patently false. It is a theory which they have superimposed on the evidence of the Scriptures, rather than drawn out from that evidence. When we study the Bible, we find inspired men, not inspired words. God mediates His word through men, with their frailty of expression and concepts. Thus it is at once both the word of God and the word of man.[8]

Like the writers of the Old Testament, those of the New Testament spoke as they were "moved by the Holy Spirit" (2 Timothy 3:16). They struggled to express in their own words the new life that had come to them in Jesus Christ. So the New Testament writings are not works of detachment or systematic theology. Rather, they are works of *witness*.

-----

[8] "The Bible is written by inspired men, but it is not God's mode of thought and expression. It is that of humanity. God, as a writer, is not represented. Men will often say such an expression is not like God. But God has not put Himself in words, in logic, in rhetoric, on trial in the Bible. The writers of the Bible were God's penmen, not His pen. Look at the different writers.

"It is not the words of the Bible that are inspired, but the men that were inspired. Inspiration acts not on the man's words or his expressions but on the man himself, who, under the influence of the Holy Ghost, is imbued with thoughts. But the words receive the impress of the individual mind. The divine mind is diffused. The divine mind and will is combined with the human mind and will; thus the utterances of the man are the word of God" (Ellen G. White, *Selected Messages*, Book One, p. 21).

We should notice a further point about the *nature* of these works. They were written to *specific situations* in the life of the first Christians. Paul, for instance, did not sit down and carefully compose a learned discourse to the believers in Galatia; rather, filled with anxiety and concern, impelled and empowered by the Spirit, he wrote a letter at white heat to save his young flock from error. When he wrote the letter to Rome, he did not face any urgent problem, but he nevertheless had in mind a particular purpose. He wrote to prepare the ground for his impending visit to that city. We could multiply examples: Luke and Acts were composed to commend the gospel to the pagan world and therefore were addressed to Theophilus; the Revelation was intended for the encouragement of the Asian churches; and so on. The point is obvious but extremely important: Each New Testament writer did his work in the context of a particular life situation in the early church.

Now the problem of "contradictions" from one writer to another begins to appear in a new light. The differences reflect the varied situations among the early Christians. Let us take a simple illustration. Suppose a father has two sons in college. One of the boys is lazy; so the father writes to him, "Work harder!" The other son is overly conscientious; so he gets a letter which says, "Don't work so hard!" If a thousand years from now an archaeologist dug up the correspondence, would he be justified in charging the father with inconsistency? Of course not.

We are now ready to consider the question of the unity of the Scriptures. From what we have noticed so far, certain misunderstandings can be swept away. First, unity is not the result of the twenty-seven documents of the New Testament being written in a special Holy Ghost language. Second, the fact that the early church gathered these books into a canon does not mean that they set out Christianity with a uniform theology.

No, the unity of the canon is *religious* and *functional*. The various writers express through a variety of forms and in a plethora of practical situations a common experience—the new life in Jesus Christ. Thus the canon sets out normative Christianity: a Christianity of variety, of checks and balances; a Christianity meeting a multitude of differing circumstances in its ongoing progress.

We may observe this functional unity of the canon in the life of the church from age to age. As the church expanded, as it entered new eras, it faced new challenges, new dangers, new difficulties. First one document spoke, then another. What was one era's "meat" became another era's "poison." But the church went on, guided and safeguarded by the canonical writings. Every one of the twenty-seven works is necessary—any will be discarded at the church's peril.

In Luther's day, the messages of Romans and Galatians were the word for the hour. This does not mean that these letters will always speak most directly to the needs of the church. Luther himself, captivated by their teachings, wished to set up a sort of "canon within the canon." He roundly belittled the letter of James as "a right strawy epistle"—although at times he was less sweeping in his condemnation. But Luther went to an extreme in taking this position. If the sixteenth-century church most needed Paul's words, the church of the following century should have heeded James' instruction.

Now we begin to understand how Matthew's Gospel may address our world with special power. It presents a particular understanding of Christianity, molded and shaped to a concrete time and place. The years have a way of bringing up the same sort of situations in the life of mankind: Man, after all, remains man—with recurrent problems, mistakes, and opportunities. So we may turn to an old familiar document like Matthew's Gospel and suddenly be struck by the directness with which it speaks to us.

Although we allow the possibility that Matthew's Gospel might be relevent to the church today, we have no guarantee that it will be so. As we look out on our world today, what is there that Matthew would address with particular effectiveness?

The Church and Today's "World"

The church today finds itself bewildered by enthusiasm. Whereas for so long we heard the plaint that the Spirit was lacking, today there seems to be a plethora of the gift.

First, the young have an upsurge of interest in Christianity. The Jesus Movement—unplanned, uncharted, and utterly unexpected—grows apace. Teenagers convert sinners on the beaches, confront the people of the night on the streets of New York, and hold mass rallies in Dallas—a Christian version of Woodstock. The organization is minimal, the music unconventional. The movement arose as a new force *alongside* the church rather than from within the church, nor has it shown an inclination to submit to the direction of the ecclesiastical hierarchy. And the church hardly knows whether to rejoice or to condemn.

Second, the secular realm has taken up the wholesale employment of Christian motifs. The barons of the entertainment world have sensed that religion is in and therefore sells. So songs about the Man who stilled the water became hits, and "Amazing Grace" made a comeback. "Jesus Christ, Superstar" was a sellout; Leonard Bernstein composed a mass (of all things!) for the inauguration of the Kennedy Center for the Performing Arts.

And the church is dismayed. Has the "world" preempted its role? Should it rejoice or wring its hands at the Christianizing (?) of the secular?

Third, there is the return of the charismatics—the men of the gifts —in the church. With the coming of the age of science, most churchmen had written off the "gifts" of the Spirit as no longer necessary: Now we have wonder drugs and insurance! But the gifts are back, and with an intensity so widespread as to be mind boggling. The most ubiquitous is also the most troubling—glossolalia. These days it is not just the Pentecostals who speak in tongues—Lutherans, Methodists, and even Roman Catholics proclaim their possession of the "gift."

So the church today finds itself in the midst of an enthusiastic frenzy: rock songs about Jesus, bumper stickers proclaiming, "One Way," mass prayer meetings, and the slippery world of glossolalia. And to this situation Matthew's Gospel speaks—and speaks with power.

We shall look closely at his document in the following chapters. We shall see how Matthew presents Jesus, his view as to what constitutes discipleship, his concept of righteousness, his teaching about the church, his understanding of time, and his perspective on the cross. At each point it will become apparent that Matthew's message comes with unusual significance in this present climate of enthusiasm.

Although our detailed study will come later, we may here set out a general characterization of Matthew's Gospel: It is "religion in overalls." Above all else Matthew's Christianity is *practical*. In an age that proclaims on its T-shirts, "Only believe" and "I love you!" (in red, white, and blue, of course), Matthew insists that practice balance one's profession, that faith and love put on overalls and get their hands dirty out where the people are—in jail, in the slums, in the poorhouse, in the charity ward.

Our world needs to know what sort of Jesus it is being offered. The church needs to heed what it means to be a disciple of that same Jesus. We must allow Matthew a hearing, for we neglect his message at the peril of a distorted or perverted view of the gospel.

Let us briefly notice how we should approach Matthew's Gospel in order to catch his message for our day.

How to "Hear" Matthew's Message

1. The simplest point is also the most important. If we want to "hear" Matthew, we must concentrate upon *his* Gospel. In practice, it is difficult to do. Most of us are used to a *composite* idea of Jesus and His teachings gathered by combining the four Gospel accounts. But the efforts of various Bible students to produce harmonies of the Gospels have only added to the problem. If we are to "hear" Matthew, we must carefully avoid filling in the details from the other Gospel writers.

Likewise we must beware of the grasshopper-style of Bible study, which jumps from one part of the New Testament to another. It serves only to blur the distinctive message of Matthew or any other New Testament writer. In the night all cats come out looking gray. We must sedulously refrain from reading Paul or John or anyone else into Matthew. We may compare and contrast but must eschew assimilation.

2. We must recognize Matthew as a writer with something to say. He is not a mere chronicler. He is an author in his own right. That has been one of the great insights to emerge in recent Biblical studies. For years New Testament scholarship occupied itself with the form-critical tasks set out by the Germans Bultmann, Dibelius, and Schmidt. Scholars dissected the text, seeking to trace its roots in the oral traditions.[9] The result was a fragmentation of the Gospels, and writers such as Matthew seemed to be no more than shadow men, collectors of the pieces. But since the work of Willi Marxsen on Mark in 1953,[10] scholars have looked anew upon the Gospels as *whole* documents. They have had to acknowledge that, while the Gospel writers employed sources for their work, they wrote with clear purposes and were not mere compilers of fragments. So Matthew, guided by the Spirit, has an *individual* presentation of the gospel for our hearing.

[9] For an introduction to form criticism, the reader might look at Martin Dibelius, trans. by Bertram Lee Woolf, *From Tradition to Gospel* (New York: Charles Scribner's Sons, n.d.). Form criticism as a method was developed immediately following the end of World War I.

[10] This new approach to the Gospels came to be known as "redaction criticism." Willi Marxsen, who coined the expression in

We have to look carefully at the way in which Matthew presents Jesus, for instance. He portrays a *distinctive* Jesus, a Jesus who speaks to the Christian situation which Matthew knows. We shall see that it will be a quite different Jesus from Mark's or Luke's or John's—or, should we say, a Jesus set forth in a particular context and for a special purpose. The differences from Mark's picture will be all the more significant since Matthew knew and used Mark's account. But it is *his* Jesus whom he wishes to present—he does not merely copy Mark.[11]

Perhaps we need to add that Matthew's Jesus will be the "real" Jesus, even as Mark's Jesus also is "real." Jesus is the Man for the church of all ages and in all climes. Any one account cannot exhaust the meaning of His life. Ever anew He comes to His church and speaks to it in the Gospel accounts.

We turn, then, to the Jesus of Matthew's Gospel. What is Matthew's Jesus, and how does he challenge contemporary portrayals of Jesus?

1954, also brought out the first full-length study of a Gospel in his study of Mark (1956). The best studies of Matthew available in English are those of Günther Bornkamm, Gerhard Barth, and Heinz Joachim Held, trans. by Percy Scott, *Tradition and Interpretation in Matthew* (Philadelphia: Westminster Press, 1963). I have drawn on the conclusions of this book fairly widely in this study. For a summary of other work in Matthew, see also Joachim Rohde, trans. by Dorothea M. Barton, *Rediscovering the Teaching of the Evangelists* (Philadelphia: Westminster Press, 1968).

[11] "The miracles of Christ are not given in exact order, but are given *just as the circumstances occurred, which called for this divine revealing of the power of Christ*" (*Selected Messages*, Book One, p. 20).

Chapter 2

Jesus: Royal Lawgiver

No Gospel writer refers to as many titles of Jesus as Matthew does. The whole range of New Testament Christology appears: Jesus is called Son of God, Son of David, and Son of man; He is King and Lord, yet also the fulfiller of the Suffering Servant prophecies of Isaiah. In two mighty affirmations of Jesus' dignity, Matthew is unique—Jesus is Emmanuel, "God with us," and He is "the Christ, the Son of the living God" (1:23; 16:16).[1]

Conceivably we might take up each of these titles and study its occurrences in Matthew. Indeed, in recent years a number of Biblical scholars have approached the Christology of the New Testament in this manner.[2] Yet is this the best way to uncover the Jesus whom Matthew sets forth? The fact that Matthew employs a title such as "Son of man" does not immediately tell us very much about Jesus. Even if we study the history of the title (its pre- and post-Matthean usage), we still have to find out what sense it holds in Matthew's writing. We have to read all around the title, as it were, in order to flesh it out. Again, Matthew may be telling us a great deal about Jesus even when he does not introduce any unusual titles. The famous fifth, sixth, and seventh chapters refer only to "Jesus" and in one verse to "Lord," but unquestionably they paint a vivid portrait of Jesus.

---

[1] The latter was Peter's "great confession," made at Caesarea Philippi.

[2] A work in English which proceeds along these lines is Reginald H. Fuller's *The Foundations of New Testament Christology* (New York: Charles Scribner's Sons, 1965).

Instead of examining titles, we shall look at three aspects of Matthew's Jesus which seem to have special significance in his presentation: the pictures of Jesus as King, as the new Moses, and as the personification of wisdom. Let us take up each in turn.

Jesus the King

The motif of kingship confronts us from the opening sentence of the Gospel. Jesus is the son of David. The long list of ancestors is designed to establish one point: the relationship of Jesus to Abraham and David so that we are ready for the Magi's question, "Where is he who has been born king of the Jews?" (2:2).

We notice particularly this kingly concern of Matthew if we compare his genealogy with Luke's—the only other one found in the Gospels. Luke also traces the line of Jesus back to David, but through Nathan instead of Solomon. Furthermore, Luke does not stop at Abraham—he goes right back to Adam (see Luke 3:23-38). Why? Because, whereas Matthew is interested in Jesus as king of the Jews, Luke wants to portray Him as *the* Man—the Man for the whole race, especially for the Gentiles.

But we have not finished with Matthew's royal genealogy of Jesus. The Jews took great interest in such lists, but this one has an unusual feature—Matthew mentions four women: Tamar, the harlot Rahab, Ruth, and Bathsheba. Why Matthew broke with custom to include these women will concern us shortly.

Matthew's account of Jesus' birth further underlines the idea of kingship. The Babe is born in Bethlehem, fulfilling the prophecy of Micah 5:2. Indeed Matthew quotes the ancient words, but with a significant variation. Whereas the Hebrew text reads, "Bethlehem, ... little among the *clans* of Judah," Matthew interprets it as "Bethlehem, ... not least among the *rulers* of Judah."

Matthew sets the birth story in the context of a clash in royal claims, made evident by the opening words of chapter 2: "Jesus . . . in the days of Herod the King . . . has been born king of the Jews." Only Matthew records the slaughter of the infants, sacrificed to the cruel jealousy of Herod the Great. Only Matthew likewise includes the visit of the Wise Men from the East. Instead of the adoration of Luke's humble shepherds, Matthew's Jesus receives gifts fit for a king. So His royal dignity is corroborated by genealogy and birthplace, by the fulfillment of Scripture, by Magi, and by star.

We are used to running Matthew's and Luke's accounts of the Christmas story together, so that manger and Magi, shepherd and star, are combined. Only when we look at the two stories separately do we begin to see the unique emphases of each. Luke has no royal genealogy, murderous threat by Herod, visit of the Magi, or star. Luke's Jesus is the Babe born in a manger, acclaimed only by shepherds—not the king of the Jews but the Man for all nations.

The motif of kingship appears in many other places throughout Matthew's Gospel. Jesus begins His preaching with the pronouncement, "Repent, for the kingdom of heaven is at hand" (4:17). Indeed, the theme of "kingdom of heaven"—its nature and conditions for entry—is on Jesus' lips throughout His discourses. (We shall study the idea of the kingdom in detail in chapter 6 of this book.) The Sermon on the Mount constitutes the magna charta of Jesus' kingdom, while His parables commence with the formula: "The kingdom of heaven is like . . ." (13:24, 31, 33, 44, 45, 47; 18:23; 20:1; 22:2; 25:1). In fact, there are no fewer than fifty references to the kingdom in Matthew's Gospel, and it must be viewed as a leading concept.

In Matthew's record of the Passion Week, the royal emphasis, so prominent in the first chapters, reappears with great force. The last week for Jesus commences with the account of His triumphal entry into Jerusalem. Down the Mount of Olives He comes, following the ancient path of Israel's rulers. Many times before He had entered the royal city, but *on foot*. Now He appropriates a colt and rides to the gates, fulfilling Zechariah's prophecy of chapter 9, verse 9: "Shout aloud, O daughter of Jerusalem! Lo, your king comes to you; . . . humble and riding on an ass, on a colt the foal of an ass."

And the crowd goes wild! Garments, palm fronds, shouts of adults, and songs of children—all proclaim that the Jews have a king again (see Matthew 21:1-11).[3]

All four Gospel writers describe the triumphal entry, but none of the others with the power of Matthew. And he alone of the Synoptic evangelists turns the reader's mind to the significance of this event by interpreting it in the light of Old Testament prophecy.

[3] "Christ was following the Jewish custom for a royal entry. The animal on which He rode was that ridden by the kings of Israel, and prophecy had foretold that thus the Messiah should come to His kingdom. No sooner was He seated upon the colt than a loud shout of triumph rent the air. The multitude hailed Him as Messiah, their King. Jesus now accepted the homage which He had never before permitted, and the disciples received this as proof that their glad hopes were to be realized by seeing Him established on the throne. The multitude were convinced that the hour of their emancipation was at hand. In imagination they saw the Roman armies driven from Jerusalem, and Israel once more an independent nation. All were happy and excited; the people vied with one another in paying Him homage" (Ellen G. White, *The Desire of Ages,* p. 570).

So the week rushes on to its finale. The final teaching recorded by Matthew is the story of the King, before whom all nations are gathered for judgment. And then comes the last, sad rush of events in chapters 25 to 27: sold by His own disciple for thirty paltry silver pieces; denied by one of His closest friends; condemned by His fellow countrymen, He stands before the Roman governor, who asks, "Are You the King of the Jews?" But the crowd wants Barabbas instead of their King! "Hail, King of the Jews!" mock the soldiers in a grim travesty of homage. They nail Him to a cross which bears the inscription: "This is Jesus the King of the Jews." From the ground below arise the insults, "He is the King of Israel; let him come down now from the cross, and we will believe in him."[4]

At last, mercifully, it is all over. Jesus' body is taken down from the cross, but even in death He is a king. Though executed with the rabble, He is given a royal burial and a royal guard at the tomb—for "the King" must stay dead!

It seems clear that Matthew sets forth a Jesus who is king of the Jews. But that is not the last word. For this king does not come with trumpet and sword. Rather, He is the king of humility.

Two passages particularly show that this is the sort of king which Matthew envisages. The opening words of the Sermon on the Mount sound out the note: "Blessed are the poor in spirit, for theirs is the kingdom of heaven." Again, when Matthew describes the triumphal entry, he quotes the words of Zechariah 9:9 with a notable omission: instead of the original "Lo, your king comes to you; triumphant and victorious is he, humble and riding on an ass," Matthew writes in chapter 21, verse 5, "Behold, your king is coming to you, humble, and mounted on an ass."

---

[4] Note how prominent is the motif of kingship in these final chapters.

Now we begin to understand why Matthew included the four women in Jesus' genealogy. Each of them, in one way or another, was misunderstood in her day, yet each was an ancestor of the Messiah. And that Messiah Himself was likewise misunderstood: The True King of the Jews, He came in humility; He was crowned with thorns instead of gold; He was acclaimed by foreigners and children instead of His own people; He was king incognito.

The New Moses

Important as the kingly aspect of Jesus is for Matthew, it is nevertheless not the most significant theme in his Gospel. Above all else he paints a picture of Jesus as a teacher, the authoritative exponent of the Law—the new Moses.

We see this point very clearly if we compare the ways in which the three Synoptic writers describe the beginnings of Jesus' ministry. For Mark, the most notable point is a *miracle* wrought by Jesus—the demoniac healed in the synagogue at Capernaum on the Sabbath. Luke, however, begins with Jesus' sermon at Nazareth in which he quoted the Isaiah 61:2 (KJV) passage of "the acceptable year of the Lord" as the prediction of the work He had come to do. Matthew, on the other hand, compresses the Marcan account in order to set forth the first major event of the ministry—the Sermon on the Mount (Mark 1:21-28; Luke 4:16-30; Matthew 5–7).

If we look carefully at the three Synoptic Gospels in turn, it becomes obvious that these accounts of the commencement of Jesus' work are programmatic for each Gospel. Thus, Mark's Jesus throughout his Gospel appears as a mighty *miracle worker*. Jesus the Teacher plays a subordinate role in Mark. For Luke, the Isaiah passage with its good news to the poor, the blind, and the captives sets the pattern for his Jesus—the friend of the outcast, the poor, the despised, and women. But Matthew's Jesus is preeminently a teacher whose mighty deeds fall into the background against the worth of His life-giving words.

A quick look at the outline of Jesus' ministry as Matthew presents it establishes the same point. We see that Matthew organizes the material around five lengthy discourses, each of which ends with a stock formula: "When Jesus finished . . ." (7:28; 11:1; 13:53; 19:1; 26:1).

Section I

4:1-25—Narrative: Introduction to the Ministry

5-7   —Sermon on the Mount

Section II

8, 9   —Narratives

10   —Discourse on Discipleship

Section III

11, 12—Narratives and Debates

13   —Discourse on the Kingdom (Parables)

Section IV

14-17 —Narratives and Debates

18   —Discourse on the Church

Section V

19-23 —Narratives and Debates

24, 25—Discourse on the Parousia

Jesus' authority as teacher is heavily underscored in Matthew's account. He alone gives us the six antitheses: "You have heard that it was said.... But *I* say to you...." Here is a new teacher, one like Moses but one who goes *beyond* Moses and the rabbis in His interpretations of Torah (the law). With devastating freedom this Jesus cuts across traditions and radically reinterprets the meaning of righteousness. (What the righteousness of Jesus signifies will concern us in a later chapter.)[5]

Throughout the Gospel, Jesus debates with the ecclesiastical hierarchy. He disputes its interpretation of the Sabbath, of the rules for lustrations, and of the relationships of Yahweh's followers to the Roman powers. He denounces the hypocrisy of its leaders with scathing words— "hypocrites," "child[ren] of hell," "blind guides," "blind fools," "whitewashed tombs," "serpents," "brood of vipers" (23:13, 15, 16, 17, 27, 33)!

We cannot overlook the remarkable manner in which Matthew closes his Gospel. It is the risen Lord who speaks, glorious in majesty, yet Matthew spares no words on description. He is concerned only with the Teacher's *command:* "Go therefore and make disciples of all nations, baptizing them, ... teaching them to observe all that I have commanded you" (28:19, 20).

The Greek construction here indicates that the basic commission is to "make disciples" by indoctrination, explaining what it means to "make disciples," and by baptism. One becomes a disciple by receiving Jesus' teaching and by baptism. Nor is this teaching merely a repetition of the Old Testament. It is "all that *I* have commanded you." We may again catch the individuality of Matthew's account if we compare it with the Marcan parallel (Mark 16:15-18).[6] Mark links baptism to a faith which produces miracles, but he does not mention Jesus' teaching! Thus Matthew's Gospel, which introduces Jesus' ministry with a teaching scene, closes on the same note.

---

[5] Note especially: 5:21, 22, 27, 28, 31, 32, 38, 43, 44. When we look closely at these passages, we see that Jesus' teaching is at times a heightening of the divine demand by extending it to embrace attitudes, desires, and motives (the first two antitheses). But it goes further than this: In the last four it either severely *limits* the old law (the third antithesis) or *reverses* it (the last three). It is clear that Jesus' words were distinguished by their *authority*.

"As Legislator, Jesus exercised the authority of God; His commands and decisions were supported by the Sovereignty of the eternal throne. The glory of the Father was revealed in the Son; Christ made manifest the character of the Father. He was so perfectly connected with God, so completely embraced in His encircling light, that he who had seen the Son, had seen the Father. His voice was as the voice of God" (Ellen G. White, *Seventh-day*

Jesus the Personification
of Wisdom

We are now able to see how Matthew's Jesus may rightly be termed the new Moses. Some scholars, it is true, have argued that the five discourses correspond to a new Pentateuch. We do not need to feel convinced of this point, however, to see the likeness to Moses.[7] The *role* of Jesus, both as authoritative interpreter of Moses and as one who goes beyond Moses, is the important matter. Other details merely fill in the picture: Like Moses, He is threatened at birth by a wicked king; He goes to Egypt and returns, in some measure recapitulating the Exodus; He proclaims the law of the kingdom from an unnamed mountain—the Sinai of the New Testament; the final picture we have of Him is like that of Moses—on a mountaintop.

Closely tied to the picture of Jesus as authoritative lawgiver is that of His role as wisdom personified. This is one of the most recent insights of Biblical studies in the Book of Matthew.[8]

Readers of the Old Testament were familiar with the view of Wisdom set out in Proverbs. Especially in Proverbs 1:20-33 and 8:1-36 wisdom is personified, calling men to walk in the way of life. During the period between the Testaments, a great interest developed in the concept of Wisdom among the Jews. Indeed, the Jewish interest was but part of a widespread concern with the topic. The tendency was to give Wisdom more and more of an independent character, to personify it as something *alongside* God, as sort of God's agent.

Adventist Bible Commentary, Vol. 5, p. 1142).

It is this note of authority which saves Matthew's presentation of law from being debased into antinomianism. "Something greater than the temple is here" (12:6). Thus Jesus is greater than interpretations and regulations, yet He is not setting the law of Moses aside. It is significant that the four antitheses which are concerned with the *application* of the Decalogue to civil life (the last four, based on Deuteronomy 24:1; Numbers 30:2; Exodus 21:24f; Deuteronomy 19:21, respectively) are those that are most radically reinterpreted. The other two antitheses are based directly on the Decalogue itself: Here the command is extended rather than reversed.

Ecclesiasticus, one of the non-canonical Jewish works of the intertestamental period, closes with these words: "Come to me, you who need instruction, and lodge in my house of learning. Why do you admit to a lack of these things, yet leave your great thirst unslaked? I have made my proclamation: 'Buy for yourself without money, bend your neck to the yoke, be ready to accept discipline; you need not go far to find it.' See for yourselves how little were my labours compared with the great peace I have found" (51:23-27, NEB*). The motifs of this passage—"Come to me," "yoke," and "great peace"— remind us of Jesus' invitation recorded only by Matthew: "Come to me, all who labor and are heavy laden, and I will give you rest. Take my yoke upon you, and learn from me; for I am gentle and lowly in heart, and you will find rest for your souls" (11:28, 29).

----

*From The New English Bible with the Apocrypha. Copyright, The Delegates of the Oxford University Press and The Syndics of the Cambridge University Press, 1976. Reprinted by permission.

An even more striking identification of Jesus with Wisdom occurs in Matthew 23:34-36. To catch Matthew's emphasis we have to read the parallel account in Luke 11:49-51: "Therefore also the Wisdom of God said, 'I will send them prophets and apostles . . .'" Matthew omits all mention of Wisdom and speaks for himself, "Therefore *I* send you prophets . . ."

Here, then, is an extension of the idea of Jesus as the Teacher. Not only is He the new Moses who imparts authoritative instruction, but He Himself *is* that new instruction.

Matthew's Jesus and Our Day

We have noticed three aspects of Matthew's Jesus: the King of humility, the Supreme Lawgiver, and the personification of wisdom. What does this Jesus have to say to the present situation of the church and society? Principally, three things.

[6] The actual ending of Mark's Gospel is in doubt; old manuscripts break off at 16:8, where the RSV has also closed the Gospel.

[7] B. W. Bacon argued that Matthew wrote a Christian Pentateuch about the New Moses who gave the New Law to the New Israel. Thus, the five discourses corresponded to the five books of the Old Testament, with chapters 1 and 2 as prologue and 26 to 28 as epilogue. H. B.

Green tried a variation on the idea, working out the five books in the first ten chapters of Matthew. The resemblances to Moses do not rest upon such forced constructions.

[8] A recent book by M. J. Suggs, *Wisdom, Christology, and Law in Matthew's Gospel* (Cambridge: Harvard University Press, 1970), brings out this point.

1. Christianity must find its base in Scripture. Matthew knew of Jesus' mighty works and recorded many of them, but apparently he also knew the dangers of setting forth Jesus as a mere wonder-worker. There was no lack of magicianlike figures in the Greek literature of the day, but Matthew deliberately avoided that pattern. At first thought, miracles are more eye-catching than words. But Matthew, guided by the Spirit, was right: Miracles evoke excitement—but excitement is often short-lived. Jesus' words, however, live on, and a Christianity founded on those words can outride all the storms of emotion which the ages churn up.

The church and the world need to listen again to Jesus' words. They need to take the yoke of His instruction, for it alone brings rest.

2. The best religion is a humble religion. Matthew's Jesus is King— of the Jews, of Israel, of the ages. But He reigns in humility, and if the church is to continue to claim Him as her Lord, she must put away her pride in her possessions (the assets of Christendom in the United States are colossal) and in her membership and practice true meekness. The kingship of Jesus leaves no place for the flippant confidence of being saved that is often paraded as the hallmark of being a Christian.

3. The Jesus of Christianity speaks with authority. In our day Jesus' message has been so diluted and deleted that no one knows what the church stands for. Often Christian leaders seem to lead the rush to every new bandwagon that rolls by. Christians are dead scared of appearing behind the times.

We must hear again the words of Matthew's Jesus and ground our lives in the uncompromising authority with which they come to us. That is the way to a personal Christianity of conviction and to a witness which will make the world sit up and listen.

So we come to the question of what the disciple of Jesus will be like. How did Matthew view the Christian life? And what can we learn from that conception?

Chapter 3

Discipleship:
In the Footsteps
of Jesus

With discipleship we come to one of Matthew's key concepts. A comparison with Mark and Luke immediately highlights this point: Forms of the word (Greek *mathētēs*) occur seventy-one times in Matthew, only forty-five times in Mark, and thirty-eight times in Luke.

But Matthew is not primarily concerned with a history of the Twelve as such. Indeed, while there are many references to disciples and discipleship, the writing contains surprisingly few references to members of the original band whom the Great Teacher had called and set apart. Instead we find the amorphous word *disciples* used over and over again. Matthew is not so much giving the story of those individuals who constituted the Twelve as setting out a definition of *the—any—*disciple of Jesus Christ. He wants to show us above all else what genuine discipleship entails and what distinguishes the true disciple from the false.

This point becomes clear as we realize that this Gospel does not limit discipleship to the Twelve. Consider the great discourse on discipleship, chapter 10, for instance. Here the Twelve are first designated as "disciples" (verse 1) but immediately thereafter as "apostles" (verse 2). Jesus is about to send them out for some field experience. After being with Him and observing His methods of ministry, they are to try their own hand at the work. He tells them where they are to go, what they should take, what they are to do and preach, and how they are to react to favorable and unfavorable receptions. But the instruction (after verse 15) goes far beyond the immediate situation facing the Twelve. It speaks of the opposition which the heralds of Jesus' message will face. They will be flogged, persecuted, and imprisoned—opposed even to the point of death. The Twelve did not meet with this hatred during the ministry of Jesus. The teaching has rather become timeless in its application, pointing to the difficulties with the Jewish and Gentile worlds that faced the young Christian church in its early stages and reaching to embrace even us. That is, what begins as instruction to the Twelve develops into a full-blown account of discipleship for every Christian.[1]

Two other great passages dealing with the life of the disciple follow a similar course. In chapter 16 Peter remonstrates with Jesus against His predictions of the impending passion (verses 21-23). The Master first rebukes Peter for not understanding the nature of His mission, but the incident provides an occasion for the teaching that a cross stamps all genuine discipleship. Although in Matthew 16 Jesus begins by speaking to "his disciples," the instruction ends up couched in terms of "whoever" and "a man" (verses 24-26).

[1] The essentially *timeless* nature of the instruction given here will become evident by a comparison of Matthew 10:16-23 with Mark 13:9-13. In the Marcan account the persecution motif functions as a specific characteristic of end-time.

Chapter 18 provides the third example. Here the context is the question of the Twelve as to who is greatest in the kingdom of heaven. Jesus answers by setting a child in their midst and telling them that unless they become like the child they will not even find *entry* into the kingdom. Once again, however, the immediate situation leads to general instruction. From the child the subject matter merges into talk of the "little ones who believe in me" and on to "your brother." The chapter becomes an important one for setting out the pattern of Christian personal relationships, or, we might say, relations between disciples of Jesus Christ.

From our quick look into chapters 10, 16, and 18 it is clear that when Jesus talks about discipleship, He does not have merely the Twelve in view. Rather, the Twelve only provide the occasion for Jesus to explain discipleship. They are themselves the first disciples and (as we shall see) examples of discipleship.

If, then, discipleship is not to be confined to the Twelve, who *is* a disciple? What features would identify him *today?*

We may conveniently approach these questions by considering in turn the disciple's relation to Jesus, the disciple as a learner, and the contrasts between the genuine and the false disciple.

The Relation to Jesus Christ

"As he walked by the Sea of Galilee, he saw two brothers, Simon who is called Peter and Andrew his brother, casting a net into the sea; for they were fishermen. And he said to them, 'Follow me, and I will make you fishers of men.' Immediately they left their nets and followed him. And going on from there he saw two other brothers, James the son of Zebedee and John his brother, in the boat with Zebedee their father, mending their nets, and he called them. Immediately they left the boat and their father, and followed him" (4:18-22).

The account of the call to discipleship is gripping in its brevity. Matthew has pared the story to the bone: "He walked. . . . He saw. . . . He said. . . . They left . . . and followed." It is a drama enacted in high-speed sequence, highlighting the principal players. The scene hinges on *command* and *response*. The word of Jesus comes as command, not as invitation, and the fishermen respond immediately. No reasoning, no bargaining, no discussion: "Immediately they left their nets. . . . Immediately they left the boat and their father, and followed him."

Now the unique relation of disciple and Master begins to come into focus. The disciple is one who has made a distinct break with the past to follow Jesus. Matthew 19:27 crystallizes the idea: "Lo, we have left everything and followed you."

What personal dynamism, what drawing power, flowed out from the Teacher of Galilee? Who can read the minds of the fishermen as they abandon their nets—and a whole way of life? We cannot read their minds, nor should we attempt to do so. Suffice it to notice that, down the ages, men and women have heard a voice—a call—and have cast aside the settled, the secure, the established, to follow that same Master into the great unknown.

Thus the relationship is unique. The disciple is tied to *Him*—not to a program, not to a philosophy, not to an organization. *He* has called, and they have left all to follow *Him*.[2]

That is why Christianity, more than any other religion to which man's questing spirit has turned, centers in a person. That is why, as no other faith does, it rests on historical events. Take away Jesus Christ, and Christianity must dwindle away. Discipleship then loses its very foundation and collapses into legalism or philosophy.

[2] Compare Ellen G. White's *The Desire of Ages*, p. 815, and *Steps to Christ*, p. 58.

A *closeness* of personal relationship exists between Jesus and disciple. The disciples' view of Jesus altogether differs from the view of the crowd. It comes across vividly in the way they address Him: Over and over they call Him *kyrios* (Lord), whereas to the others He is no more than *didaskalos* (Teacher). (Incidentally, only Matthew's Gospel preserves this careful distinction. Compare 8:25; 9:28; 13:51; 14:30; 16:22; 17:4 with 22:16.)

Jesus is their Lord. They are *followers* of Him. If one word preeminently describes the personal relationship of discipleship, it is *followers*.[3]

The position of a follower offers a mixed blessing. At times the consequences are pleasant; at others they are painful.

On the one hand, following Jesus brings a closeness to Him. All through Matthew's Gospel, the disciples are continually *with* Him. Where He goes, they go; as the tremendous and finally tragic events of the ministry unfold, they are always *there*. "And when he got into the boat, his disciples followed him"—this is the pattern of the Gospel (8:23). They are present to hear His words—some are addressed to them (e.g., the Sermon on the Mount, 5:1). They see His miracles. They hear the forecast of His rejection. They dine by His side at the Supper, their final meal together before His death. They are with Him at the arrest in the Garden. And the very last words of the Gospel are addressed to them.

---

[3] In fact, the word *follow* occurs at least fourteen times with reference to discipleship in Matthew. It is used a total of twenty-four times in the first Gospel. We see clearly the *attractive* power of Jesus Christ in Matthew's Gospel.

On the other hand they share the hardships of Jesus' ministry. To the would-be disciple, the scribe who is quick to promise, "Teacher, I will follow you wherever you go," Jesus replies, "Foxes have holes, and birds of the air have nests; but the Son of man has nowhere to lay his head" (8:20). Again, in the great discourse on discipleship, the perils and pains of the follower come into sharp focus, as we have already noticed. "If they have called the master of the house Be-elzebul, how much more will they malign those of his household." "He who loves father or mother more than me is not worthy of me; and he who loves son or daughter more than me is not worthy of me" (10:25, 37).

Pleasure and pain are the lot of the follower. The famous saying of chapter 11:28-30 combines both ideas. It is the *yoke* to which the disciple bends his neck—not a very pleasant idea. But it is no ordinary yoke: "my yoke is easy, and my burden is light."

We may notice a final point concerning the unique relationship which is at the heart of Christian discipleship: *imitation*. Following Jesus is essentially a recapitulation of His life and words.

Chapter 10 emphasizes this aspect. The disciples must bear the same message which Jesus preached: "The kingdom of heaven is at hand"! They go in His name and in that name repeat the mighty deeds of His ministry—healing the sick, raising the dead, cleansing the lepers, exorcising the demons. They go out as His representatives. "He who receives you receives me." And, in the Great Commission which closes the Gospel, it is not their own words but "all that I have commanded you" which they are to teach men to observe, as they, like their Lord before them, "make disciples."

Sharer of His secrets, companion in His labors, participant in His sufferings—this is the disciple of Jesus Christ. He enjoys a relationship closer than the ties of blood, dearer than links of race and country, education, or profession. Listen as the Lord of the disciple describes it: "While he was still speaking to the people, behold, his mother and his brothers stood outside, asking to speak to him. But he replied to the man who told him, 'Who is my mother, and who are my brothers?' And stretching out his hand toward his disciples, he said, 'Here are my mother and my brothers!' " (12:46-49).

The Disciple as a Learner

Despite the closeness of the disciples to Jesus, they have much to learn. Indeed, the Lord has not called them to follow Him because they show spiritual maturity. Just as the Twelve were undistinguished in Jewish society, so their continuing sinfulness after their call is stressed by Matthew.

The most dramatic demonstration of their weakness occurs in the Garden. Although Jesus had sought to prepare them for the coming conflict with His adversaries, at the time of test they all "forsook him and fled." Yet all through his Gospel Matthew readies us for this great act of disappointment. Repeatedly Jesus has rebuked their lack of faith: "O men of little faith" (6:30; 8:26; 14:31; 16:8). Also the stronger "O faithless and perverse generation, how long am I to be with you? How long am I to bear with you?" (17:17).

We find them rebuking the children who were brought to the Lord for a blessing. We see them striving among themselves, angry lest James and John hold places of precedence among them. Despite the Lord's warnings of their impending failure and His admonition to "watch and pray," they all fall asleep in Gethsemane. And the mob that comes out armed with swords and clubs to arrest Jesus is led by Judas, one of their number!

Jesus' own designations of His followers likewise accent their continuing weakness. "Little ones," He calls them, and even "babes" (10:42; 18:6, 10, 14; 11:25). These affectionate terms show at once His tender regard for them and their utter dependence upon Him.

And He *is* concerned for them. They are weak, but they are learners in the finest school man may attend, the school of Jesus Christ. To these same "babes" is given the hidden things of God, secrets which "the wise and understanding" might have had (11:25). These "little ones" are identified with Him, and God notes every act done to help them. They are like the scribe of 13:52, who is "trained for the kingdom of heaven." Each of the five great sermons which structure the Gospel is directed toward them, and those words will perfect them!

The account of the feeding of the five thousand illustrates sharply this aspect of the disciple. Jesus has spent the day healing the sick in a lonely place, where a great crowd has gathered to seek His aid and to see His mighty acts. But the day is ending, and the disciples grow restless. It is time for the meeting to break up and for Jesus to send the people home to supper. But when they at last give voice to their feelings, they receive a surprising reply: "They need not go away; *you* give them something to eat" (14:16). Here Jesus tosses the ball back into the disciples' court! His words are as impossible as they are unexpected.

Yet eventually the disciples *do* give the crowd their supper. They receive the broken bread and fish from Jesus' hands and distribute them to the multitude. From being weak and doubting, they become partners with Jesus.

Such is the life of the disciple. His weaknesses are great. He has no "holier than thou" faith or experience in which he may boast. The pressure of what Paul calls "the flesh" is always there: its striving for the top place, its misunderstanding of the meaning of the cross, its roughness, and its cowardice. How much he needs his Lord! But that Lord knows him and has called him as he is, with all his deficiencies. That Lord who has called is with him always, even unto the end of the age. And so, by continual association with the Lord, by continual exposure to the living words of the Teacher, the "little one"—ever weak, ever in need—is ever learning.[4]

True Versus False Discipleship

While Matthew's Gospel has much to say on the subject of discipleship, he also occasionally sounds a discordant note. Here and there Matthew tells us that not all discipleship is genuine. One may claim to be a follower of Jesus but be rejected by the Lord Himself.

This idea comes to expression very clearly in chapters 7 and 25. In the first passage we find people who address Jesus as "Lord" and who recount their prophesying, exorcism, and many other "mighty works." But the awful sentence falls upon them: "I never knew you; depart from me, you evildoers" (7:23). The second passage relates the parable of the sheep and the goats—the disposition of mankind at the last great assize. Once again we catch the element of *surprise*. Those who are on the left hand, who hear the fateful word, "Depart from me, you cursed, into the eternal fire prepared for the devil and his angels" (25:41), are stupefied that Jesus should thus judge them.

---

[4]"There are those who have known the pardoning love of Christ and who really desire to be children of God, yet they realize that their character is imperfect, their life faulty, and they are ready to doubt whether their hearts have been renewed by the Holy Spirit. To such I would say, Do not draw back in despair. We shall often have to bow down and weep at the feet of Jesus because of our shortcomings and mistakes, but we are not to be discouraged. Even if we are overcome by the enemy, we are not cast off, not forsaken and rejected of God. No; Christ is at the right hand of God, who also maketh intercession for us. Said the beloved John, 'These things write I unto you, that ye sin not. And if any man sin, we have an advocate with the Father, Jesus Christ the righteous.' 1 John 2:1.

"And do not forget the words of Christ, 'The Father Himself loveth you.' John

From these passages we can see several negative characteristics in a definition of discipleship. Most obvious, of course, is that of *profession*. Merely taking the name of the Lord does not in itself qualify one to be a disciple. It is Jesus, not man, who designates the disciple. Second, *Christian service* in itself does not prove discipleship. From a human viewpoint, surely exorcism, miracle-working, and prophecy evidence a relationship with the Lord—but not from God's! Even those who are supremely confident of their standing with the Lord may hear the terrible "I never knew you." Finally, and here we look at Jesus' denunciation of the religious leaders of His day, *outward show* does not characterize the disciple. Indeed, those who most vaunt their religiosity are least likely to be the Lord's.

So much for the pseudodisciple. But can we go beyond what we have already discovered in this chapter to further characterize the genuine? What *positive* features of true discipleship does Matthew set out?

We briefly note four features which mark genuine discipleship: practicality, humility, performance of the divine will, and understanding Jesus' words.[5]

True discipleship issues in acts of practical Christianity. Discipleship is *lived* out rather than preached out. Just as grapes don't grow on thorns, nor do figs on thistles, so a living relationship with the Lord will bring its good "fruit."[6] Indeed, the genuine follower of Jesus may live largely unnoticed by his fellows, even by his brothers in the church. He does not keep any score of his good deeds. He is not trying to win "brownie points" with the Lord. But day by day his discipleship shows, and the Lord takes note. Every one of those "little, nameless, unremembered, acts of kindness and of love" described by Wordsworth—the food to the hungry, the visit to the sick, the help to the prisoner—evidences that he is indeed a follower of Jesus Christ.

16:27. He desires to restore you to Himself, to see His own purity and holiness reflected in you. And if you will but yield yourself to Him, He that hath begun a good work in you will carry it forward to the day of Jesus Christ. Pray more fervently; believe more fully. As we come to distrust our own power, let us trust the power of our Redeemer, and we shall praise Him who is the health of our countenance" (*Steps to Christ*, p. 64).

[5] "How could He show that a mere profession of discipleship did not make them disciples, or insure them a place in His kingdom? How could He show that it is loving service, true humility, which constitutes real greatness?" (*The Desire of Ages*, p. 644).

[6] Notice Matthew 7:16-20, given in the context of true and false discipleship. Luke has a similar saying (13:23, 24). Matthew's

Second, the disciple of Jesus knows that humility is true greatness. He knows that the desire for the applause of the crowd, grasping for the spoils of office, and all those subtle words and deeds by which men seek to put down another and raise themselves have no place in the kingdom of God. "It shall not be so among you," says his Lord, "but whoever would be great among you must be your servant, and whoever would be first among you must be your slave; even as the Son of man came not to be served but to serve, and to give his life as a ransom for many" (20:26-28). If the Lord willingly took the lowest position, so also must His follower.

Third, the genuine disciple is alert to God's will. Not *man's* estimate of him but *God's* will is his passion, for he who does the will of the Father enters the kingdom. Says the Lord, "Whoever does the will of my Father in heaven is my brother, and sister, and mother" (12:50). So the divine will is exalted above human ideas of right and wrong, greatness and servitude.[7]

Finally, the true disciple understands Jesus' words. "He who has ears, let him hear" (13:9). The common crowd hear, but hear not; they see, but see not; but to the disciple is "given to know the secrets of the kingdom of heaven" (13:11). To them alone is given the scene of glory on the Mount of Transfiguration and to them the mysterious words, heavy with portent, of the coming sufferings of their Lord. The knowledge which they gain is not a ground for boasting, even as it does not entitle them for a part in the kingdom. Rather, it is a privilege which they gain as a result of the closeness of their relationship with the Lord. As we share our confidences with our friends, so the Lord shares His secrets with those who are closest to Him.

account considerably expands the statement about the "narrow" way and adds a group of sayings which emphasize the *practice* of genuine Christianity. In this way he sharply rebukes antinomian tendencies.

[7] This is surely at the heart of the idea of bearing the cross (see 16:24-26). The cross stands for *death*—the death of the self-life, the selfish ambition, the will which seeks to live apart from God.

With this word we have returned to the beginning of our study of discipleship. Truly the special relation of disciple and Lord undergirds every other aspect of the disciple's life. Because of his personal closeness to Jesus he is able to be a learner although weak, he can practice humility in a world of self-assertiveness, he can know and do God's will, and he can recapitulate Jesus' life of gentle and loving acts in a predatory environment.

We may now see clearly how Matthew's concept of discipleship applies in our day.

The Disciple Today

As the twentieth century draws to a close Christianity is big business. The assets of the churches are enormous. If you can preach well enough, you can make a lot of money—and fast. At the same time we see a rash of charismatic manifestations—healings have become respectable and even the Catholics are speaking in tongues. The big emphasis is on the Spirit.

At such a time as this Matthew's concept of discipleship seems peculiarly relevant. If his words mean anything, they tell us that genuine discipleship cannot be gauged by outward manifestations.

I may be a famous preacher,
I may even win many souls
   for the Lord.
I may be able to raise up
   the sick by my prayers.
Even the devils may yield
   to my command!

But God may not call me
   a disciple!
Or, on the other hand—
I may be considered
   a model citizen.
At church I'm in good
   and regular standing.
I support all worthwhile
   community projects.
People like me are
   the backbone of the nation—
   honest, hardworking, and
   law abiding.

But the words may fall upon my shocked ears, "I never knew you!"

Is it possible? All those good works? All those prayers? All those sermons? All those powerful displays of the Spirit? The Spirit— what about the Spirit?

Possible, says Matthew's Gospel— possible and likely, for *God* alone knows who is the genuine disciple. He alone designates him, and the divine decision brings with it many surprises. In its essence discipleship involves something that man can't see. We may fool our friends, even our wife and children, but *discipleship involves the heart.* God alone can read it, He knows how it has responded to His call. He knows how deceitful it is—yes, deceitful enough to trick even the preacher himself! But His call has come. In some that call has fallen like seed on the good ground. It has sprung up to bear good fruit.

The question is, Have I, like those men of old, left all to follow Him? Have I so yielded my will and my ways over to His plan that my life is no longer my own? Yielded— no matter what the cost! Perhaps we need to be reminded that, even in these days, the follower of Jesus will find pain as well as pleasures as he seeks to walk in Jesus' footsteps.

But His word still has power. That voice is yet heard—and many, like those fishermen by Galilee, immediately leave their boats and nets to follow. Their Master is King in humility, so why should they seek great things for themselves? They are weak, but He is a Mighty Teacher—and they are ready to learn.

And most and best of all, to Him they say from the heart, "Lord!"

Chapter 4

Conduct: Better Righteousness

High in the Himalayas you can meet them—pilgrims trudging toward the headwaters of the sacred Ganges. Down in the heat of the plains you may find others, turning over and over, measuring their length over hundreds of miles along the route to holy Benares. Or you may come across a Jain of the strictest sect of his religion—a digambara, "sky clad," that is, stark naked. He has renounced even clothing in his religious zeal. He walks along, sweeping the ground before each step, lest he crush the merest form of life underfoot.

Christianity, too, has its devotees. Even if today people don't perch for years on a pillar like Simeon Stylites, many still flee the world for the confines of the cloister. Renouncing friends and family, marriage and mammon, they search their souls in the endeavor to please a demanding deity.

What does God require? That question has haunted men and women through the centuries. Would the Lord be pleased with a thousand sheep, with ten thousand rams? What if—what if man should give his most precious possession, if he should even go to the nth point of religious devotion and offer up his firstborn as a sacrifice? Surely that would please deity! No, said the prophet Micah, turning the scale around to a moral set of values, no sacrifice, no gift is what God requires. The statement in Micah 6:6-8 is surely the highwater mark of the religion of the Old Testament.

In Matthew 5:20 we meet again this searching question of the ages. We meet it headlong, for Jesus' words thunder in our ears: "Unless your righteousness *exceeds* that of the scribes and Pharisees, you will never enter the kingdom of heaven." And not only there. Righteousness, in fact, is a major concept of Matthew's Gospel. In its various forms it occurs twenty-eight times, whereas we find it only twice in Mark and seventeen times in Luke.

Furthermore the following cursory list shows the *weight* which Matthew's Gospel assigns to the concept:

3:15 Jesus Himself undergoes baptism that He might fulfill all righteousness.

5:6 The disciple is one who hungers and thirsts for righteousness.

13:43 The righteous will shine forth like the sun in the kingdom of God.

25:31-46 The parable of the sheep and goats shows God's decision of righteousness.

27:24 Jesus is called a "just [righteous] man."

Clearly righteousness is the great goal to be sought by the follower of Jesus Christ. "Seek first his kingdom and his righteousness" (6:33). But *how?*—that is the question. On this point there is controversy among Biblical scholars. To some, Matthew with his passion for righteousness is a legalist, because he seems merely to set out the requirement without giving the way to do it. They say he is ignorant of Paul's teaching that faith in Jesus Christ meets God's demand for righteousness. Either ignorant of Paul—or in controversy with Paul. Is Matthew writing to correct a Pauline misunderstanding of the Christian life?

We must study very carefully the matter of righteousness in Matthew. It is only fair to let him speak on his own terms. We should not try to read Paul into Matthew or set up Matthew against Paul. It will help if we consider the topic in three stages: Matthew's basic concept of righteousness, the meaning of the "better righteousness," and the relation of Matthew's concept of righteousness to Paul's.

The Basic Concept

What is the *essence* of righteousness for Matthew—a way of thinking, a relationship, a particular state or status? None of these. Over and over as we look at the occurrences of the word and its cognates we are impressed that righteousness is focused in *conduct*.[1]

Perhaps the parable which designates "the righteous" in chapter 25 best underscores the point. What they have *done* is the crucial element—their acts of kindness and mercy, their thoughtful and unselfish ministry to the unfortunate. Contrariwise, the failure to perform such deeds calls down the King's wrath on the unrighteous. The teaching surely is too plain to be gainsaid. Judgment proceeds on the basis of man's deeds.

Yet we find the same idea everywhere. The opening verse of chapter 6 warns against "practicing your piety," doing righteousness, in an ostentatious manner. The verses immediately following elaborate what these acts are: almsgiving, prayer, and fasting. Again, we recall the eighth beatitude of chapter 5—the blessing on those persecuted "for righteousness' sake." What is it that brings down the ill favor of the world? Not some inner state, not a relationship, not a feeling. No—it is the *life lived* by the citizen of the kingdom of heaven which sets him apart from society around him. The Lord has touched and changed his life, and it cannot be hidden. Persecution will never be far away.[2]

[1] Compare Ellen G. White's *Christ's Object Lessons*, pp. 312, 313:

"Righteousness is right doing, and it is by their deeds that all will be judged. Our characters are revealed by what we do. The works show whether the faith is genuine.

"It is not enough for us to believe that Jesus is not an impostor, and that the religion of the Bible is no cunningly devised fable. We may believe that the name of Jesus is the only name under heaven whereby man may be saved, and yet we may not through faith make Him our personal Saviour. It is not enough to believe the theory of truth. It is not enough to make a profession of faith in Christ and have our names registered on the church roll. 'He that keepeth His commandments dwelleth in Him, and He in him. And hereby we know that He abideth in us, by the Spirit which He hath given us.' 'Hereby we do know that we know Him if

In chapter 5, does not verse 20, a crucial one, point also to conduct when it speaks of the "better" righteousness? It is not here a question of the righteous or the unrighteous. There is no discussion as to whether or not the religious leaders are righteous. They are righteous—but not righteous enough! And once again the elaboration of this verse is in terms of better conduct: "You have heard that it was said. . . . But *I* say to you." The better righteousness will be manifested in the way we react to the man who insults us, by our relations to people of the other sex, by faithfulness to our marriage partner, by the words that fall from our lips, by the way we handle a situation of hostility and wrong done against us.

So we might continue. Whether it is Jesus coming to the Jordan and submitting to John's baptism "to fulfil all righteousness," whether it is John himself coming to men "in the way of righteousness," whether it is Jesus' disciple being counted righteous by his words—throughout we detect the same note. Righteousness in Matthew's Gospel is intensely and primarily *practical* in its character. Righteousness is inseparable from conduct.

Yet we have not quite covered Matthew's concept of righteousness if we leave it there. Righteousness —but *why?* Righteousness is tied to conduct—but on what grounds? We shall see an important extension of the concept by pursuing these questions.

54

we keep His commandments.' 1 John 3:24; 2:3. This is the genuine evidence of conversion. Whatever our profession, it amounts to nothing unless Christ is revealed in works of righteousness."

[2] See Ellen G. White, *Thoughts From the Mount of Blessing*, p. 29:
"So it is with all who will live godly in Christ Jesus. Between righteousness and sin, love and hatred, truth and falsehood, there is an irrepressible conflict. When one presents the love of Christ and the beauty of holiness, he is drawing away the subjects of Satan's kingdom, and the prince of evil is aroused to resist it. Persecution and reproach await all who are imbued with the Spirit of Christ. The character of the persecution changes with the times, but the principle—the spirit that underlies it—is the same that has slain the chosen of the Lord ever since the days of Abel."

And soon we note significant conjunction of "righteousness" and "kingdom." For instance:

5:10 Those who are persecuted for the sake of righteousness receive the kingdom.

6:33 The disciple is to seek first God's kingdom and God's righteousness.

13:43 The righteous will shine like the sun in their Father's kingdom.

13:49 The righteous are to be separated from the evil at the end of the age (verse 47 terms the passage a parable of the kingdom of heaven).

25:34, 46 The righteous inherit the kingdom.

Here, then, is the idea of righteousness in Matthew's Gospel. It is *conduct in view of God's kingdom.* Righteousness does not involve merely good works, not simply building a reputation for clean living. No, it is far more. It is righteousness with a new dimension, a righteousness as radical as the kingdom which calls it forth. To seek the kingdom is to do the righteousness on the fulfillment of which one may gain admission to the kingdom. The life of the righteous man shows conduct in harmony with God's will—conduct well pleasing to Him in the age of the kingdom.

And there at the head of the righteous stands that Righteous Man! He Himself has *lived,* has *acted,* has *produced* a life well pleasing to God. So, entering the ranks of sinners, He has done righteous acts for them. As was His baptism—"to fulfil all righteousness"—so was the entire life. The kingdom has come, and He has brought it with and by His acts of righteousness!

Now we are prepared to grasp the teaching of the better righteousness.

The "Better" Righteousness

The attempt to understand Jesus' term has usually proceeded along one of two lines. On the one hand, scholars have held that Jesus here juxtaposes an external type of righteousness to an inner, moral one. That is, whereas the pharisaic effort was essentially legalistic, the new righteousness demanded by Jesus was one of the heart. On the other hand, other scholars have argued that the failure of the Pharisees was due to their hypocrisy. They taught and told others but failed to live out their own precepts.

But does either of these explanations—legalism or hypocrisy opposed to the righteousness demanded by Jesus—really satisfy the criteria of Matthew 5? A careful examination of the passage shows that both are inadequate.

For a start, it is clear that, if anything, the better righteousness is *more* "legalistic"! Six times the word comes: "You have heard that it was said . . ." and six times it is followed by: "But *I* say to you . . ." In each case there is not a lessening of the requirement but rather an enhancement. The commandment against murder is expanded to include anger and strained personal relations. The prohibition against adultery now includes the enticement, the lustful eye. The rule against divorce is widened so that divorce is limited to the single ground of unfaithfulness. Oaths are forbidden altogether. Instead of retribution, personal injury must be accepted gladly. Love of the neighbor is widened to include even the man who seeks one's ill will.

Nor can it be said that the difference lies in an internalizing of the old commands. True, the range of the law is now extended to include the motive (the angry feeling, the lustful thought), but the emphasis, as we already noticed, is still on conduct. The concern is how I *react* to the one who bears me a grudge, to the sight of a pretty face, when my marriage begins to suffer stress, when I am unjustly handled or abused. No, what is in view here is the *total* man—his thoughts, feelings, and actions amid the pressures and challenges of day-by-day living.

Likewise the matter of hypocrisy is not at all the point. In chapter 23 this charge is leveled against the Pharisees, but we are not to import the content of that chapter into this setting. The six antitheses are not, "The Pharisees do . . . but I say." No, it is not a case of the Pharisees versus Jesus, but Moses versus Jesus. What we have is the new Moses calling into question the very foundation of the old righteousness, calling it into question and over-turning it by the force of His own personal authority. Not hypocrisy, not legalism, but a totally new demand is surely the nature of the better righteousness of Matthew 5.

We may grasp the concept if we consider the way of righteousness set out by the Pharisees in Jesus' day. Christian thinking tradition-ally has branded these men as legalists, hypocrites, and even worse—those who plotted the mur-der of Jesus Christ. In all fairness we ought to notice that Pharisaism was not as bad as Christians have usually made it out. The Pharisees earnestly sought God's will and meticulously observed the law.

The *law!*—after the Babylonian captivity, *that* was the tilt taken by Judaism. Torah in all its forms, written and oral, became its pride and joy, its overriding concern, its guiding light, its focus of study. And the Pharisees, along with the scribes, were the experts in the law.

In Matthew 23 we see a sharp example of rabbinical scrupulousness. The Pharisees, said Jesus, tithe even the garden herbs—mint, anise, cummin. They were concerned preeminently with good works, with racking up a record that would count in their favor in the books of God. Conduct likewise was their watchword in the pursuit of righteousness. And here was the crux, laid down by the rabbinate: The good deeds must exceed the evil deeds. In the balance sheet of each life there were plus and minus columns, and the righteous man would be he whose plus account outweighed the minuses![3]

The Pharisees earnestly attempted to please God, to know His will in every detail, and to follow it. But, said Jesus, that did not suffice. Unless the follower of Jesus could find better righteousness than this, he could not enter the kingdom.

How could this be? How could one be more intent on obedience than the rabbinate? If the demands for righteousness were lifted still higher, would not righteousness become an utterly distant goal, quite out of mankind's reach?

Yet, even before Jesus, such a demand had been made among the Jews. Among the Dead Sea sectaries—those isolationists who had chosen to drop out from Jewish society—we find just such a criticism of the rabbinate. Among the scrolls which they left and which miraculously came to light in our day, we find this critique: The Pharisees are "the seekers of smooth things." The Pharisees were not too strict in their seeking for righteousness, but rather not strict enough!

[3] The Mishnah (Aboth 3.16) records this teaching.

A parallel demand comes from Jesus Christ. The righteousness of the Pharisees will not suffice to enter *His kingdom*. There it is—the kingdom! A new age is dawning and with it old norms are swept aside. What was good enough for father will no longer do—the "old time religion" will be left out in the cold. The new kingdom calls for a new ethic.[4]

The goal is now higher than any Pharisee had dared set it. The words sound like hammer blows upon our wondering ears. "You, therefore, must be perfect, as your heavenly Father is perfect" (5:48). We draw back in amazement. Can it be that the whole ball game has been changed, that man's thinking and efforts of the past need throwing out? What is this—no longer a set of rules, a codified norm of conduct to be meticulously spelled out and followed, but God Himself as the norm? Man like God! What could be more radical than this?

Thus the better righteousness of the Sermon on the Mount is not better than the old because it is of "the heart" instead of "the hand." Nor is it better because it is practiced instead of being merely proclaimed. No—it is better because it is a righteousness that matches the nature of Jesus' kingdom. As that kingdom is utterly unlike any kingdom made or dreamed of before or since, so the lives of its citizens are to be a demonstration of righteousness such as Judaism and the world have never witnessed. In a word, that righteousness is to mirror the righteousness of God Himself.[5]

[4] See *Thoughts From the Mount of Blessing*, pp. 54, 55.

[5] See *ibid.*, p. 77.

Matthew and Paul

Matthew and Paul have the most to say about righteousness in the New Testament. The expression "God's righteousness" is the key to understanding the argument of Paul's letters to the Romans and the Galatians (e.g., Romans 1:17; 3:5, 21, 22, 25, 26; 10:3). It was out of the struggle to discern the meaning of that expression by a professor of theology in Wittenberg University that the Protestant Reformation was brought forth. Matthew does not have the combination "righteousness of God," although he has much to say about the unqualified righteousness. But, as we have noticed above, his setting out of the better righteousness leads inexorably to a similar position—man's conduct (righteousness) is to mirror the divine conduct (righteousness).

There the similarity between Paul and Matthew seems to end, however. Whereas Romans and Galatians stress the *availability* of God's righteousness (as a free gift, accepted by faith),[6] in Matthew we find only the *demand* for it. We seem to have the requirement without the means, the goal without the power. Matthew has raised his sights higher than even the rabbinate but has left us dangling in frustration before an unattainable ideal.

Such observations have led many Protestant scholars to a low view of Matthew. They have set him out as essentially Jewish in his thinking, an Old Testament man in the garb of Christianity, one whose concern with conduct pleasing to God knows nothing of that faith which leads to justification of the ungodly.

But is this denigration of Matthew's understanding of Christianity just? Is it fair to portray him a superlegalist, one who out-Pharisees the Pharisees?

---

[6] See, e.g., Romans 4:5: "And to one who does not work but trusts him who justifies the ungodly, his faith is reckoned as righteousness."

Perhaps it is time for us to stand back and take a broader view. Unfortunately Protestants, because of the extraordinary part played by Romans and Galatians in the genesis of the Reformation, have come to set up these documents as the touchstone of their faith. But look at the whole New Testament: These two letters stand somewhat alone in their emphasis. Look even at the total Pauline correspondence: Again they are apart. Indeed, I think we might rightly hold that Romans and Galatians are unrepresentative of Paul's letters—certainly less representative than the correspondence with Corinth. Indeed, if Romans and Galatians are to be made the criterion, quite a few other documents of the New Testament seem to have missed the gospel along with Matthew!

I do not in any way seek to lessen the significance of Romans and Galatians in their historical place and their role for Christian life today. I merely suggest that we maintain a *balanced* view. And such a view is likely to be more charitable toward Matthew's presentation of Christianity, more ready to hear him on his own terms, for Matthew *does* have a presentation of the gospel. It is certainly not Paul's, but it is the gospel nonetheless. Let us notice three significant points.

The first comes from one of Jesus' strangest parables—the story of the laborers in the vineyard, found only in Matthew 20:1-16. Here is a story that turns every human dealing on its head. Several groups of workers go out in turn to labor as they are hired throughout the day. Those who commence at daybreak have a contract to receive a day's wage for their work. The others, being hired later, do not expect such a reward. Some are sent out to work as late as 5 PM, when only an hour remains, but they are glad for at least a little work.

Then come sunset, tools down, and the paychecks. Those hired last are paid first, and surprise!— the boss gives them a full day's wage. Yes, even those who worked for only an hour get a full twelve hours' reward. Those who have sweated in the sun all day see it, and their mouths begin to water —they are in for a fat paycheck. But again, surprise!—they get just the same, the regular day's wage. Understandably they begin to complain about it to the boss, but he only replies, " 'Friend, I am doing you no wrong; did you not agree with me for a denarius? Take what belongs to you, and go; I choose to give to this last as I give to you. Am I not allowed to do what I choose with what belongs to me? Or do you begrudge my generosity?' So the last will be first, and the first last" (20:13-16).

No human business works like this. The unions would never allow it. Doesn't the story even seem offensive to our sense of justice? What sort of world would it be if we acted so capriciously?

If *we!* But the story is not about man, but about *God*. It isn't a paradigm for human business concerns but instead is a revelation of "the kingdom of heaven." And when we look into the story closely, what do we see? Once again, the triumph of the gospel. Instead of human law, we see the rule of grace. Instead of salvation as reward, we see the generosity of a loving God who freely gives to those who simply trust in His goodness and go out to work for Him. Those who work for reward, those with their eyes on the paycheck and their minds on their own efforts, end up disappointed, while those who labor without thought of reward, merely trusting their Master, receive beyond their wildest hopes.

Is not this the essence of the gospel? Does not this concept deliver Matthew's Gospel from legalism, no matter what its detractors may say?

The second point reinforces this parable. We noticed it in the last chapter—the note of *surprise* that marks the final accounting of men's lives at the Great Assize. Both in the brilliant passage of 7:19-21 and the judgment scene of chapter 25, man's *claim* is contrasted with God's sentence. Both groups—those designated as righteous and those called evil—are amazed at the divine verdict. And again all legalism collapses. There can be no thought, Matthew tells us, of man's *claiming* entry to the kingdom by the force of his own deeds.

The final point carries us a step farther. Only at the judgment does God *pronounce* men righteous. Before the judgment, righteousness is to be sought after, to be hungered and thirsted for, as the beatitude describes (5:6). The satisfaction comes afterward—and as an eschatological gift. So we find the word of 13:43, which again pictures the lot of those who receive the divine approval at the final dispensation of mankind: "Then the righteous will shine like the sun in the kingdom of their Father."

These three points—grace over law, surprise, righteousness pronounced—deliver Matthew's Gospel from legalism. In his own way Matthew arrives at the concept of righteousness by faith.

So we ought to lay aside the alternative, Paul *or* Matthew. Both present the gospel. Both are correct. Both are geared to different situations in the life of the church. The church today needs both.

If we had only Romans and Galatians, the church might fall into the pit of antinomianism and libertinism. Even in Paul's own day he had to resist these logical—but false—extensions of his message. And Luther, rediscovering that message, likewise faced the problem of libertinism among his followers.

On the other hand, if we had only Matthew we would have a deficient view of faith—that faith which is counted to us for righteousness. We could easily be led toward a legalistic stance in the Christian life.

Matthew's Concept of Righteousness Today

We have mentioned the need for both Paul and Matthew in the life of the church. But as I see it, it is perhaps Matthew rather than Paul who needs to be heard at this time.

Why? Principally because our generation has become obsessed with the ideas of freedom and love. Under the cloak of these terms a good deal of nonsense is being bandied about as Christianity. The currents that swirl in society always affect the presentation of the gospel—indeed it must be so for it to command a hearing. But therein lies the danger—that the preacher will reflect what men want to hear instead of calling them back to God's demands.

Matthew's voice sounds out like John the Baptist's in the modern wilderness. Amid the "I'll do as I please" babble, he tells us that high ethical concerns and conduct will mark the Christian's life. Loose living and lax morals in the name of Christian liberty are a travesty of the gospel of Christ.

The bitter cry of many young people in this land is that the church has become part of the Establishment. And it is not unjustified. Sad to say, we are often more concerned with public image and good relations than with matters of morality, but an overriding regard for the status quo means death to the ethical powers. No wonder many young people turn off to Christianity and turn on to the cults from the East or become involved in the radical politics of the New Left.

Further, Matthew would tell us that ordinary norms of "good living" cannot suffice for the kingdom of Jesus. He comes to man with a radical demand, sets up a requirement which is as spectacularly different as the nature of His kingdom. The way of the kingdom is a new way, a better way. Man no longer is given a set of rules to follow in order to please God; rather, he is to act in his sphere as God acts in His.

Faced with the high claims of the Sermon on the Mount, let us not try to dilute them. Let us not try to get around them by rationalization and theologizing. This has been the cop-out by Christians over the centuries. Only when we fully recognize their *radical* nature do we do justice to them.

Then we see very clearly that the way of the kingdom is not the way of man left alone in his humanness. No government has ever adopted it. There have never been any "Christian nations" according to its terms. It stands apart from the way of the world, calling for such a transformation of conduct that man has tried to reject or rationalize it. It is so demanding that even legalism begins to quake before it, for what is the point of a legal requirement if it is so exalted as to be beyond all that man might hope to attain? The gate of salvation becomes narrow indeed.

Legalism may quake, but legalism is not called for. This is the final word in Matthew's concept of righteousness: All our righteousness is in God's hand. Whereas righteousness is the quest of the disciple, and whereas the judgment is the time of vindication of the righteous, that righteousness is a *pronouncement,* not a reward. It is a free gift, not an earned wage.

So, in the life of the disciple, marked as it is by a conduct like God's in the midst of a careless world, the ultimate triumph is one of grace. He who hears the call of the kingdom and, trusting its Lord, seeks to live by its demands—this is the righteous man of Matthew's Gospel.

Chapter 5

The Church—in the Storm-tossed Sea

Early Christian thought likened the church to a ship. Tossed by the waves of a hostile society, buffeted by winds of hardship and false teachings, the bark of the new religion looked very frail. Many times it seemed threatened to plunge to a watery end.

Matthew also employs the ship symbolism for the church. Indeed, as we shall see, he draws his picture of the storm-tossed boat of Christianity with peculiar poignancy. Yet his Gospel is concerned with the church in a manner far beyond the use of this symbolism. It is, in fact, something in the nature of a manual of instruction for the administration of the church.[1]

An ancient catechism from the first century of Christianity has been preserved. Called the Didaché (i.e., "the teaching"), it certainly is no later than AD 110 and may be as early as AD 80-85. Its resemblance to the first Gospel is striking,[2] and Matthew may well belong to the same type of writing (but Matthew is, of course, far more. It is a Gospel, not merely an extended catechism).

Matthew's Gospel is also unique in its use of the term for church—*ekklesia*. The term occurs in the controverted passage of chapter 16: "You are Peter, and on this rock I will build my church" (verse 18). Because the passage strongly underscores the authority of the church, it has embroiled Protestants and Catholics in fierce discussion about the primacy of Peter.

---

[1] K. Stendahl, in his *The School of St. Matthew* (Uppsala, 1954), argues that the first Gospel is not really a Gospel at all (in the sense that Mark's is) but rather a manual of doctrine and administration for the church.

[2] The Didaché sets out a code of Christian morals under the heading of "The Two Ways." Parts of it are taken directly from Matthew's Gospel. It also gives simple authoritative directions about fasting, prayer, the Lord's Supper, the treatment of visiting Christians, contributions, worship services, and church officers.

It is true that Matthew does not set out any systematic doctrine of the church. The great expressions for the church found in the epistles, such as "saints," "elect," "true Israel," and so on, do not occur. Nor does it mention any officers of the church—bishops, elders, and deacons. But from what we have indicated above, the Gospel is vitally concerned with the church. If it has no *explicit* ecclesiology, it certainly does have an *implicit* ecclesiology.

Bringing Matthew's underlying concept of the church out into the light is our task in this chapter. Once again it will help if we approach the topic in terms of its most prominent aspects: the church and judgment; the church and authority; the church and privilege. We shall take up each in turn.

The Church and Judgment

Two striking parables found only in Matthew's Gospel best describe the relation of the church to God's judgment: the stories of the wheat and the tares and of the dragnet, both found in chapter 13. We should look at them in some detail.

The "weeds" of the first parable probably refer to the plant known as bearded darnel. This species closely resembles wheat, even to the "bearded" character of the heads of grain.[3] Wheat and darnel grow side by side, and it takes the acutest eye to spot the difference. For months they flourish together, and the task of distinguishing them is difficult. But a change comes. As the summer days draw on, the true nature of the darnel shows up. Instead of the golden ears of grain, only black heads appear.

[3] The Greek *zizanion* probably indicates the *Lolium temulentum* (darnel). Darnel grows in grain fields and resembles wheat. The seeds of the darnel (which are black) are poisonous.

The intent of the parable is clear. First of all, we notice the *mixed* character of the church. Obviously not all in the church are God's—there are "the sons of the evil one" as well as "the sons of the kingdom." Further, it is *difficult* to distinguish the two groups. It is not the task of the church to set up an internal investigating agency that will establish genuine credentials. Indeed, the parable seems to teach that any such human judgment will likely fall into error, wrongly assigning a son of the kingdom to the ranks of the evil one. Rather, only the final judgment will reveal the identity of all, and then not a human edict but the word of God issues the verdict.[4]

For Matthew's Gospel it is evident that God's church is a *church facing the judgment*. Mere membership in the church by no means guarantees citizenship in the kingdom at the end of time.

The parable of the dragnet reinforces this thought. The kingdom of heaven is like a net which draws people of all types into its sweep. Once again it is only at the "end of the age" that the separation into good and bad occurs, and that task is not given to human minds.

A church facing the judgment! Matthew's Gospel flings aside all presumptuous security, all resort to human values and reputations. Already we have seen how it discards as invalid the appeal to miracles, to impressive acts of Christian service. As no other document in the New Testament, it strips man of his boasting.

In a similar vein it sweeps away all hope based on descent. "Do not presume to say to yourselves, 'We have Abraham as our father'; for I tell you, God is able from these stones to raise up children to Abraham," declaims the Baptist (3:9). There can be no appeal to father or grandfather, just as no lobbyist, pressure group, or agent with an "inside track" to the divine ear may be found to push a person into divine favor.

[4] Ellen G. White, *Christ's Object Lessons*, pp. 72, 73.

Instead, each disciple faces the tests of the judgment alone, and those tests are the same for all: (1) the "fruits of repentance" (3:8; 7:19); (2) the will of the Father (7:21); and (3) the better righteousness (5:20).

There is a further aspect of this matter of the church and judgment, however. The parables of chapter 13 might lead us to hold that God has *predetermined* those who are His sons and those who are not. Then the judgment would be merely the *disclosure* of the two groups. Men might be surprised, but God all along would have known those who were His.

Such a view is not correct. Matthew's Gospel teaches that the identity of good and bad is not fixed prior to the judgment. There is the *possibility* of one's moving from one category to the other. Only at the judgment will membership in the categories be fixed for all time.

The repeated admonitions to watchfulness plainly lead to this observation. The great eschatological discourse of chapter 24 runs into the parables of Matthew's next chapter. Each of these—the ten virgins, the talents, and the sheep and the goats—highlights the need for faithfulness in the Christian way.

The problem of the five girls who fail to gain entry into the marriage is that they were "foolish"—they failed to make the needed preparation—not that they had been chosen to be among the doomed. Likewise the condemnation of the one-talent individual is in his own lack of courage and resourcefulness. Timidity and laziness eventually meant that he lost the one talent he had received. There is a close similarity with the five foolish girls. All had *opportunity,* all were members of the church, but they failed to improve the opportunity given them. Thus the judgment would find them wanting—and so cast out. The final parable (the sheep and goats) strongly reiterates the idea of unfulfilled possibilities.

Here, then, is the first aspect of the church in Matthew's Gospel. It is a solemn idea, one that should cause each professed follower of Christ to pause and take stock. Membership in the church is not necessarily coterminous with participation in the Messianic community at the end-time, for the church itself comes into judgment!

We move to the second distinctive feature of the Matthean ecclesiology —the authority of the church.

The Church and Authority

Over the course of the centuries the Matthean statements concerning the authority of the church have served as the center of controversy. They are three: 16:19, 18:18, and (to a much lesser degree) 28:18. We shall consider each in turn, noticing both the nature and the limitations of the authority envisaged in these passages.

Chapter 16 makes the strongest statement of the three. "I will give you the keys of the kingdom of heaven, and whatever you bind on earth shall be bound in heaven, and whatever you loose on earth shall be loosed in heaven," says Jesus after Peter's "great confession" at Caesarea Philippi. The words seem unequivocal.

The concept implied here profoundly influenced the shape of European history. No matter how powerful the state, the church was armed with a weapon before which the most powerful monarch would tremble—the authority of excommunication. In an age when heaven seemed closer to the earth than today, when religious matters were at the forefront of discussions and of any philosophy of life, the threat of exclusion from eternal hope was a serious matter. Thus we see a king like Henry IV humbling himself and pleading for the pope's forgiveness. He treks across the Alps in midwinter, and the pope keeps him waiting out in the snow for three days before he will grant him an audience![5]

[5] Note the account in *The Great Controversy,* pp. 57, 58.

But we do well to look again at Matthew's words in chapter 16. It seems remarkable that the *setting* of the famous statement should so often have been disregarded, *for these words are given in the context of the suffering of the earthly Jesus.*

Immediately after the statement concerning ecclesiastical authority, Jesus foretells His impending passion. Peter rebukes Him: "God forbid, Lord! This shall never happen to you" (16:22). But Jesus thrusts Peter aside. He is a hindrance. He stands on man's side instead of God's. Then, in verses 24 to 27, Jesus speaks of the cost of discipleship. The way of the follower of Jesus is the way of the cross. Whoever would save his life will lose it, but whoever loses it for the sake of Jesus Christ will surely find it.

We can now see the great contrast. Chapter 16 is not a blanket authorization for papal power—for arrogant high-handedness in the name of Jesus Christ. Far from it. The church's authority—for its authority is indubitable—is subject to the example of the life and suffering of the earthly Jesus. It is a church which imitates the lowly life of her Lord, a church which takes up His cross in its shame and abuse and yes, even its death, which is vested with His authority.[6]

How different would have been the history of Christendom if it had followed Matthew 16 in its entirety. Authority without humility, the keys without the cross—it was a horrible distortion of the intent of the gospel.

---

[6] I am indebted to Günther Bornkamm for this insight, which I consider to be of great value. See *Tradition and Interpretation in Matthew,* p. 48: "The church after Easter with its life and the office of the keys sanctioned by Jesus, is thus subjected to the law of the life and suffering of the earthly Jesus. If the decisions made by the Church are to be valid in the coming judgment it is clear that the forgiving and retaining of sins is thereby placed under the same standard as that of which 16:24-27 speaks: imitation in suffering and life-devotion."

In 18:18 we find the second statement of church authority: "Truly, I say to you, whatever you bind on earth shall be bound in heaven, and whatever you loose on earth shall be loosed in heaven." Once again, however, the statement comes in a setting of lowliness. Indeed, the disciples have been arguing as to who is the greatest in the kingdom of heaven, and the words of the Lord come as a rebuke. Unless they are changed and become like a little child, they shall not even *enter* the kingdom. He goes on to speak about the "little one"—the disciple, as we noticed in our study of discipleship. How weak he is, how frail! Then comes a discussion of relations between disciples and the statement of verse 18.

Again we conclude that there is no warrant here for ecclesiastical pretensions. The church is vested with the authority of her Lord only as she walks in the way of His lowliness.

The final statement comes from the words of the risen Christ which close the Gospel: "All authority in heaven and on earth has been given to me" (28:18). The assertion is unequivocal. *All* authority is in Jesus' hands. On the basis of that right, His followers must go to the ends of the earth, making disciples of all nations. "Making disciples," we noticed earlier, entails two aspects—baptizing and imparting all that Jesus had commanded. Not the words of Moses, not the teachings of the prophets, not the understanding of the Christian religion gained by its first adherents—but the words of Jesus. Again we cannot fail to catch the overriding note of authority in these words.

Christianity is not to be propagated apologetically. We do not stand, hat in hand, nervously rubbing our hands together, as we proclaim Jesus Christ. We go out to make followers for Him among men of all races on the basis of the authority vested in Him as Lord of all. And that authority is to last "to the close of the age."

But we note: It is the authority of *the Lord* which Matthew here brings out so strongly. There is no abdication of authority to His would-be servants, no setting up of human institutions and officials which may take His name and then claim the right to speak as they please. No, indeed; a *strict limit* is placed on the office of the disciple. His authority is not his own. He merely goes out in the name of his Lord. Nor is he free to add or to take away. He is to teach *all that his Lord has commanded.*

We may close our discussion of this aspect of the church in Matthew's Gospel by suggesting that two extremes in ecclesiastical authority have come into view. On the one hand, there is the extreme which would so deny or limit the authority of the church that it is reduced to a merely human society. Then it is no better and no worse than a political or social institution —and then, too, it really has nothing significant to say. Matthew sweeps away such a view. *The church has authority because it is the church of Jesus Christ.*[7] On the other hand there is the extreme of ecclesiastical high-handedness in the name of Jesus Christ. Then, Matthew's Gospel reminds us, the church has authority *only as it remains the church of Jesus Christ* —that is, only as it continues in His way of lowliness and suffering.

We are now ready for the third aspect of the church—its privileges.

[7]Compare Ellen G. White's *The Acts of the Apostles,* p. 122: "Thus Jesus gave sanction to the authority of His organized church, and placed Saul in connection with His appointed agencies on earth. Christ had now a church as His representative on earth, and to it belonged the work of directing the repentant sinner in the way of life.

"Many have an idea that they are responsible to Christ alone for their light and experience, independent of His recognized followers on earth. Jesus is the friend of sinners, and His heart is touched with their woe. He has all power, both in heaven and on earth; but He respects the means that He has ordained for the enlightenment and salvation of men; He directs sinners to the church, which He has made a channel of light to the world."

The Church and Privilege

The privileges of the church are multifaceted. We may think of them in terms of special *benefit* and special *service.*

While God is gracious toward all the creation, He confers special benefit on those of the church. They are called "sons" (17:26)—a term of endearment and familial status. In a peculiar way, then, the church is the sphere of divine relationships and divine activity. The sons share in the secrets of the kingdom (13:11), and they witness fulfillment of the expectations from ancient times (13:16). So there is closeness to the Father which only those of the church may know. It is a society of those who have been touched by the divine hand, who have transposed their allegience from the affairs of this life to the service of the kingdom.

That is the second aspect—a special service. Three striking metaphors highlight it—salt, light, and leaven. The church, we may say, is God's agent on earth. It is the theater of His grace, the channel through which the divine purposes find fulfillment. In salt, light, and leaven the active power to *transform* society is indicated. What God *is,* so is the church to be. What He *does*, so is the church to do.

Matthew raises service to the level of unique privilege. God yields His operations to human agencies, depending on them for the accomplishment of His work on the earth. If the salt loses its flavor, if the light is hidden, if the leaven loses its power, then apparently in each case the world will be so much the worse, and God's activity will not have been done.

God manifested through the church! Can it be possible? This indeed is the teaching of the special service of the church. The light of the church is so to shine in the world that men will glorify *the Father in heaven.*[8]

---

[8] See *ibid.*, pp. 13, 163: "Wonderful is the work which the Lord designs to accomplish through His church, that His name may be glorified."
"God has made His church on the earth a channel of light, and through it He communicates His purposes and His will."

It is a glorious concept—but also one which makes the heart tremble. Like Paul we exclaim, "Who is sufficient for these things?" The church—how frail, how insignificant, how puny it seems! How ready are the ideologies of the age to silence it! How intent are political systems to crush it! How foolish it looks before the wisdom of the world. And so much at fault—rent by divisions, slow to respond to the call of the Spirit, often unsure of its direction and its aims. Can *this* be the agent to manifest the Divine in the world? Has not the Almighty again humbled Himself as He did when He stooped to the manger of Bethlehem?

We can appropriate the concepts of the church only by faith. The idea of the church is too daring for reason to assent to and too foolish for wisdom to acknowledge.[9]

But this *is* the Matthean concept of the church. And now, perhaps, we can better appreciate the picture that Matthew has left us of the church as a frail craft alone on the storm-tossed sea.

Mark and Luke, as well as Matthew, recount the story of the stilling of the storm, but the telling has a peculiar slant in Matthew's Gospel which clearly makes it far more than a miracle story. The contrast emerges plainly if we compare Matthew 8:23-27 with the parallels in Mark 4:36-41 and Luke 8:22-25. In the Marcan account, we note in turn the description of the storm, the disciples' words, "Teacher, do you not care if we perish?" the rebuke to the wind, the immediate calm, and the challenge to the disciples, "Why are you afraid? Have you no faith?" Mark tells the incident in a simple, direct way so that the accent falls on the miraculous aspect. The same holds true for the Lucan passage. It basically reiterates Mark's story.

[9] See Ellen G. White's *Selected Messages,* Book Two, p. 396:
"We should remember that the church, enfeebled and defective though it be, is the only object on earth on which Christ bestows His supreme regard. He is constantly watching it with solicitude, and is strengthening it by His Holy Spirit" (Manuscript 155, November 22, 1902).

But not so in the Matthean account. The passage, unlike the parallels in Mark and Luke, is set in the context of *discipleship*. The key word *follow* links the account with 8:18-23: " 'Teacher, I will follow you.' . . . And Jesus said, . . . 'Follow me.' . . . His disciples followed him." Likewise the storm here is no ordinary wind squall: The Greek *seismos*, literally "earthquake," pictures a cataclysmic upheaval. Further we notice a difference in the words of the disciples. They cry out, " 'Save, Lord; we are perishing.' " Now Jesus speaks *before* acting and rebukes them, " 'Why are you afraid, O men of little faith?' " then calms the storm.

It seems undeniable that Matthew tells the story in such a way as to speak with special meaning to the early believers. The account is now much more than a nature miracle. It is a picture of early Christianity. It elaborates what it means to follow Jesus. There is the little church, fearfully buffeted by the upheavals of the Roman world, apparently about to be swallowed up by the hostile society. From a human viewpoint the end seems near—the little ship cannot survive —and the cry of Jesus' followers is one of utter desperation. But the Jesus whom they seek to follow is Lord of the church. Despite the fragility of their faith, and even in the midst of perils, He is near to speak the delivering word.[10]

It vividly pictures the life of the church. To follow Jesus is hazardous —no "flowery beds of ease" here! But it is also one of supreme privilege. The church is not a mere human institution. It is *His* church. And because He is her Lord, He will not forsake her, no matter how great her perils.

[10]Günther Bornkamm first brought out the manner in which Matthew's account of the stilling of the storm is directed toward the life of the early Christian church. This was in an article first presented in 1948 and reproduced in *Tradition and Interpretation in Matthew,* pp. 52-57.

Matthew's Concept of the Church and Our Day

While in many respects the church never had it so good as today, in others it has fallen on hard times. In the United States the church is a big business with huge assets. It even has a notable political clout: we aren't yet ready to elect an avowed atheist to the White House. But, amid all the prosperity, ominous signs appear on every side.

Perhaps the supreme problem of the church is its loss of "cool." The church is unsure of itself. It seems to have lost its identity. Despite its assets and political clout (or could it be *because* of these things?), a crisis of the spirit besets it. Here is the fear—that the church is more and more irrelevant in the modern age.

It is a fact that the church no longer enjoys the respect of society which it once had. Many people are openly suspicious of what the church is about. They see it as a conservative, vested interest. It is likewise true that the church has trouble attracting the brightest minds to its service. Time was when the community looked up to the minister as its natural leader, when the leading sons of the family aspired to enter pastoral service. No more. Very often the church has to rest satisfied with dropouts or rejects from such status professions as medicine and science. It is an ominous sign.

The church finds itself buffeted by the winds of Biblical criticism, by the storms out of scientific laboratories, and by the earthquake from psychology and psychiatry. So much that used to lie within the province of the church seems to have been explained on naturalistic terms that the church itself seems ready to be explained away.

At such a time as this we need to catch Matthew's concept of the church. We need to sense the *glory* of the church. *It is the church of Jesus Christ!* It is the church which He claims as His in a unique way, and it is upon the church that He showers the special privileges of His grace. Even if many moderns have ridiculed the church, it is God's.

Nor should we lightly treat the *authority* of the church. It is the custodian of Jesus' words, and it is empowered with rules of order and discipline. If medieval man was too much awed by this aspect of the church, surely modern man has gone to the other extreme. We need to catch again the *seriousness* of church membership. The church isn't another club to jump in and out of as fancy dictates.

Perhaps, above all else, we need to be reminded of the *lowliness* of the true church. Only as we reflect the life of the Man of Galilee do we have the right to be called His church. Only as we look at Him and away from every human device, only as we discard our pride and pomp, our love of display and money, should we take His name. Only as we realize that we too—yes, *we*—not just the drunkard, the gambler, and the harlot—must come into judgment, will we turn from our own ways and seek the better righteousness of Christ's church.[11]

The ship in the storm-tossed sea—how the waves mount up! How the earth heaves! The church is almost engulfed. But that Lord who has watched over the boat through the centuries is still near. He hears the cry of fear and answers the most fragile faith. The church is His, and therefore it will not—for it cannot—go down![12]

---

[11] I am indebted to John R. Jones for the following helpful observations concerning the role and stance of the church today. He says, "Do you think the church's servanthood might today provide as much of the answer to secular challenges as does her glory? Maybe one of the values of the Woes section for Matthew was the way in which it permitted the church to sweep aside the attitudes of superstition and tradition which enslaved men and which still evoke the world's scorn of 'conservative, vested interest,' and released her to minister to the real needs of men: the cup of water no less than the teaching and baptizing.

"It seems to me that the authoritarian stance was a function of the church's catering to her adherents' need for psychological security before God so that a major reason for the demise of this stance has been the modern rejection of that particular way of answering the need. Some, who still accept the category of the sacred, meet that need through direct divine evidence, e.g., glossolalia. And of course Matthew is opposed to such enthusiastic misappropriation. . . . For others today, who live wholly within a secular frame of reference, any such quest for security is disallowed. To these I suppose even our most ringing affirmations of the church's glory must fall on deaf ears. But a *serving* church? That still bears an intelligible witness to the secular challenge. I don't mean by this that the church has no agenda but that which the world proposes, but that like Matthew's Jesus (who in chapter 10 instructs His emissaries to first go out meeting the people's *perceived* needs), she always *starts* there. Then her glory isn't tied to triumphalism, but it is vested in her servanthood."

[12] It is worth noting the high place given the church in the writings of Ellen G. White. We simply list the following as examples: the church is carried on Christ's heart (*Christian Service,* p. 243), is a case which contains God's jewels (*Testimonies,* Vol. 6, p. 261), is Christ's channel of communication (*The Acts of the Apostles,* p. 122), is Christ's fortress in a revolted world (*Medical Ministry,* p. 89), is Christ's representative on the earth (*The Acts of the Apostles,* p. 122), is the dearest object on the earth to God (*Christ's Object Lessons,* p. 165), is God's appointed agency for saving men, is God's city of refuge (*The Acts of the Apostles,* pp. 9, 11), is God's property (*Testimonies to Ministers,* p. 19), is Heaven's appointed channel for revelation of God to men (*Thoughts From the Mount of Blessing,* p. 40), is the repository of the riches of Christ's grace, is the theater of God's grace (*The Acts of the Apostles,* pp. 9, 12).

Chapter 6

The Kingdom— Already But Not Yet!

"Time, like an ever-rolling stream, Bears all its sons away." We are all borne along in that stream. The current is swift—and cold! It is futile to try to fight it, though some of us make the attempt. A whole consumer industry capitalizes on the effort to swim against the stream, or at least to arrest its rapid pace. So we have cosmetics, wigs, and hairpieces; we can get a facial or a face-lift; and there are pills to rejuvenate.

But all to no avail. Life has two certainties—taxation and death. The one indubitable fact of our existence is that it will one day come to an end. We shall be cast up on the bank of an alien shore while the cold tide rushes past us.

Time is a great mystery. It is not a thing to be grasped. It has no objective reality. We glibly speak of it, just as we bandy around incomprehensible terms such as "eternity" and "nothingness." But time cannot be reduced to any satisfactory concept, although we tend to regard it on the analogy of space. Time is the measure of our existence. It is the relentless drumbeat of life. It tells us that we are *here* but that we will not *always* be here. What we are—what all things are—will inevitably cease.

In our age we have become slaves of the clock. The chronometer stands as our crowning achievement and the hallmark of our folly. We have come to codify existence by figures on a dial, by the sweep of a mechanical hand. But this view is patently false. Life is *lived*. We must not reduce it to mechanics. Some hours fly by with the wind, others drag with leaden feet. Why? Because, while we have grown accustomed in this twentieth century to look to gadgets for reality, our existence can never be so confined.

With these insights we can turn again to Matthew's Gospel and study his ideas about time. But as we shall see, it is not of time per se that the Gospel speaks. Rather, the philosophy of time comes to expression in a concrete image—"the kingdom." It is a rich symbol, one that will amply reward us if we probe its secrets.

Before we take up the "kingdom" motif, however, we shall try to see the view of history that Matthew holds so that we can better appreciate the peculiar nature of Jesus' kingdom—a kingdom that *already is* but has *not yet* come in its fullness.

Matthew and History

The clue to grasping Matthew's concept of history inheres in a phrase which occurs with slightly varied wording twelve times—"that it might be fulfilled" (1:22; 2:15, 17, 23; 8:17; 12:17; 13:35; 21:4; 26:54, 56; 27:9, 35). Jesus' entire life, ministry, and death are comprehended under this idea. His birth, His flight to Egypt, His youth in Nazareth, His ministry of healing, His gentle, unobtrusive compassion, His teaching, His final entry into Jerusalem in triumph, His rejection and seizure, and His betrayal are all set forth as the enactment of Old Testament prophecy.

In chapter 2 of this book we noticed how Jesus is the New Moses. We observed also the genealogy of Jesus set out in Matthew 1—fourteen generations from Abraham to David, fourteen more from David to the deportation to Babylon, and a final fourteen from Babylon to Jesus. Indeed, we may say that the entire Gospel of Matthew rests on the Old Testament and grows out of it. There are continual correspondences, a continual looking back to the period of the people of old for hints of and allusions to the meaning of Jesus Christ. To mention but one further example: the two Josephs. Like the Joseph of old, the husband of Mary is a dreamer. God instructs him in a dream to marry Mary (he had resolved to break the betrothal when he found out that she was pregnant). He is warned in another dream of the evil plans of Herod the Great. He returns from Egypt in response to a dream. The decision to settle down in Galilee instead of coming back to Bethlehem is due to yet another dream warning (1:20; 2:12, 19, 22).

The story of Jesus is not merely one of correspondence to Old Testament anticipations however. "That all things might be fulfilled" points the Christ-event as the *climax* of the Old Testament. It is as though the whole period up to the time of Jesus is one of waiting for the realization of the Hope of Israel. In other words, Jesus is the Man of the ages. His coming marks the watershed of history.[1]

We mark the flow of time by that coming. The division of history into BC and AD genuinely reflects the Matthean philosophy of history. Jesus' appearance on earth cleaves history in two. All before is promise, hope, anticipation; all after is the era of the Son, He who is with us always, even to the end of the ages. No wonder the genealogies end with Him!

83

[1] "With profound and reverent interest the elders of Israel should have been studying the place, the time, the circumstances, of the greatest event in the world's history—the coming of the Son of God to accomplish the redemption of man. All the people should have been watching and waiting that they might be among the first to welcome the world's Redeemer" (Ellen G. White, *The Great Controversy*, p. 313).

Yet there is a final word to be said. The birth, life, ministry, and death of Jesus mark the fulcrum on which the ages turn, but they are not themselves uniform. That is to say, within the actual coming of Christ there is a qualitative distinction. The years prior to the commencement of ministry, for instance, Matthew passes over without a word. Then when the ministry begins, there is evidence of *movement,* of the inexorable march of events toward the denouement. At Caesarea Philippi the end is foreshadowed: "From that time Jesus began to show his disciples that he must go to Jerusalem and suffer many things from the elders and chief priests and scribes, and be killed, and on the third day be raised" (16:21). So Jesus' life and work rushes to its paradoxically sad, yet glad, climax. Of the twenty-eight chapters in the Gospel of Matthew, eight deal with that climax.[2] At last it is all over. A cross stands high on Golgotha, and the inscription reads, "This is Jesus the King of Jews."

Thus, BC better stands for "Before the *cross*" rather than the generalized "Before Christ," because at Calvary, in one unique act, history reached its climax. Existence—that flow of experiences in the stream of time—can never be the same again.[3]

From what we have said here it follows that Matthew's Gospel takes history *seriously.* Jesus' life is not a grand ideal. Calvary is not a glorious idea. *Jesus was real. Calvary was real.* Matthew is not concerned with writing a philosophy or a theology. He is vitally interested in *something that happened*— something without parallel, without repetition. It is a something that has invested history with meaning.

Now we are better prepared to take up the strange expression which Jesus often used—"My kingdom."

[2] All the Gospel writers show a similar concern with the final week of Jesus' life. Thus Mark devotes 6 out of 16 chapters to it; Luke, 6 out of 24; and John, no less than 10 out of 21!

[3] "The cross of Calvary challenges, and will finally vanquish every earthly and hellish power. *In the cross all influence centers, and from it all influence goes forth. It is the great center of attraction;* for on it Christ gave up His life for the human race. This sacrifice was offered for the purpose of restoring man to his original perfection; yea, more. It was offered to give him an entire transformation of character, making him more than a conqueror" (*Questions on Doctrine,* p. 661).

The Kingdom of Jesus

According to the Gospel of Matthew, Jesus spoke of the kingdom of heaven no fewer than fifty times. When we compare this with only two references to the church, we better understand the force of Goguel's observation that Jesus preached the kingdom of heaven, and the church was the result! Indeed, it is startling to see the manner in which *kingdom* is almost wholly confined to the Gospels. It practically disappears as soon as we move into Acts and the Epistles. *Church*, on the other hand, occurs but twice in the Gospels (the two Matthean references), but is a dominant motif of the following documents.

The kingdom idea is not one which appeals to the modern mind. After a couple centuries of liberal democracy, we find it archaic and even distasteful. Even in those nations of the West where kings and queens still reign, they have no effective power. They are monarchs without a kingdom, mere figureheads.

What, then, did Jesus mean when He spoke of His kingdom? The first problem to be tackled is whether He distinguished the "kingdom of God" from the "kingdom of heaven." The expressions occur about equally in Matthew. It seems, however, impossible to make out any significant difference between the two. On the other hand the following passage suggests that He used the expressions interchangeably: "And Jesus said to his disciples, 'Truly, I say to you, it will be hard for a rich man to enter the kingdom of heaven. Again I tell you, it is easier for a camel to go through the eye of a needle than for a rich man to enter the kingdom of God'" (19:23, 24).

But kingdom does not have to signify an actual domain, a political realm. Failure to recognize this has led to many misconceptions in the past and still today clouds the understanding of the topic. The Greek *basileia* can as well be translated as "reign" or "rule"; that is, the "kingdom of God" signifies the "divine rule," or the "reign of God." When we catch this point, we see that Jesus was not a political enthusiast whose aspirations for a new Davidic kingdom were thwarted by His own tragic death. Rather, we see that in His life and work God's reign was breaking through. In Jesus something divine was happening.

This understanding of the kingdom—that it represents the reign of God breaking in upon human society—becomes clearer when we consider the *time* aspects of the kingdom. We shall see that, according to Jesus, the kingdom *already has come* in His ministry, but that in some way it is still future—not yet!

If "kingdom of heaven" parallels "kingdom of God," then what is the basic content of that kingdom? Did Jesus expect that His work would usher in an actual physical, territorial kingdom? There are some students of the Bible who have thought so. The most famous of them was Albert Schweitzer, the great doctor, interpreter of Bach, theologian, and missionary to Lambarene. Schweitzer held that Jesus believed an actual political kingdom would result from His preaching and that, when it did not eventuate, Jesus gave Himself in a last desperate effort to install it at Jerusalem.[4]

[4] The final section of Schweitzer's great work, *The Quest of the Historical Jesus*, paints such a picture of Jesus. More recently, S. G. F. Brandon in *Jesus and the Zealots* has sought to link Jesus to revolutionary activity in first-century Palestine.

The Kingdom Come

Matthew sets forth John the Baptist as a preacher of the imminent kingdom. "Repent, for the kingdom of heaven is at hand," he proclaimed from the wilderness of Judea (3:2). It is a message of urgency: Time is very short, the wrath is about to fall, and the One mightier than John will soon appear.

As Jesus commences His ministry, He repeats that call: "Repent, for the kingdom of heaven is at hand" (4:17). His opening words in the Sermon on the Mount are: "Blessed are the poor in spirit, for theirs is the kingdom of heaven" (5:3). Indeed the whole sermon is about the kingdom. It is a manifesto of the privileges and responsibilities of its citizens. Clearly, the kingdom was not far in the future. The kingdom *even now* is dawning. Jesus is imparting instruction for the "now" time.

Matthew 12:24 provides an especially telling scene. As the opponents of Jesus witness His mighty acts, they denigrate them with what appears to be a plausible objection—"it is only by Be-elzebul, the prince of demons, that this man casts out demons." Jesus answers their challenge headlong. Will Satan then destroy himself? By whom do the sons of the Pharisees succeed in their exorcisms. Also by Satan? Then comes the clincher: "But if it is by the Spirit of God that I cast out demons, then the kingdom of God *has come upon you*" (12:28). The statement is unequivocal. Jesus' miracles evidence that God's rule has broken through to mankind.

The inquiry of the Baptist from prison offers a parallel case. John wishes to know if Jesus really is the promised "coming one," or if that one is still in the future. Jesus' reply is significant. The disciples of John should report what they have seen and heard—the blind restored to sight, the lame walking, the lepers cleansed, the deaf hearing, the dead raised up, the poor receiving the Good News. Once again the appeal is to Jesus' mighty works—the works of God's reign.

Later in this chapter we find a further statement of the inbreaking of the kingdom. Says Jesus, "From the days of John the Baptist until now the kingdom of heaven has suffered violence [or, "has been coming violently"]. . . . For all the prophets and the law prophesied until John" (11:12, 13). The verse as it has come down to us is obscure, but not in its teaching concerning the kingdom. Clearly, John is set forth as the *beginning* of the reign of God—the Old Testament revelation was "until John."

As with Jesus' miracles, so with His teachings. His preaching is specifically termed "the good news of the kingdom" (4:23; 9:35). Likewise, over and over He commences His parables with, "The kingdom of heaven is like . . ." Nor can it be said that these parables refer primarily to the future. Rather, the reverse seems to be the case. Usually they set out the character and growth of that reign of God inaugurated by Jesus' ministry. Consider but one example—and a well-known one at that—the parable of the sower. After Jesus has told the parable, He tells His disciples, " 'To you it has been given to know the secrets of the kingdom of heaven' " (13:11). Then, as He explains the parable, He reveals that the seed is the hearing of "the word of the kingdom." It seems beyond dispute that the application of the parable is not to some future realm. The accent is on the here and now. The kingdom is breaking in, and Jesus' preaching is the Good News of the fact.

Yet we must quickly add that Jesus was far more than a mere announcer. It was *in His person* that the kingdom was coming—in His mighty acts and teachings that God's reign was breaking upon the people who long had sat in the darkness and shadow of death. With the coming of Jesus the kingdom had come.[5]

The Kingdom to Come

Although God's reign was present in the work of Jesus Christ, it clearly has a future aspect also. The Lord's Prayer itself embodies this aspect. For two thousand years Jesus' followers have prayed, "Thy kingdom come" (6:10). By this they intend, "May Thy kingdom come." It recognizes that God's reign is not yet manifested in fullness.

It has become fashionable among many scholars of the Gospels to set aside or diminish the futuristic aspect of the kingdom. They have set out a teaching of "realized eschatology"—that Jesus' life and ministry themselves removed the need of any future coming in of the reign.[6] But this interpretation cannot be made to square with the Lord's Prayer or, indeed, with the New Testament as a whole. And Matthew's Gospel, possibly more than any other document of the canon, preserves this future.

---

[5] Note the following statements along this line:

"As the message of Christ's first advent announced the kingdom of His grace, so the message of His second advent announces the kingdom of His glory" (*The Desire of Ages*, p. 234).

"The Saviour's mission on earth was fast drawing to a close. Only a few months remained for Him to complete what He had come to do, in establishing the kingdom of His grace" (*Christ's Object Lessons*, pp. 253, 254).

"The kingdom of God's grace is now being established, as day by day hearts that have been full of sin and rebellion yield to the sovereignty of His love" (*Thoughts From the Mount of Blessing*, p. 108).

[6] The writings of C. H. Dodd are especially associated with this idea. Apparently

In earlier chapters of this book we have come across futuristic aspects repeatedly. We noticed how often the themes of kingdom and judgment are interlinked, with judgment unquestionably still to come. Again, there are those passages which speak about the state of blessedness in the kingdom. Matthew 8:11 tells how "many will come from east and west and sit at table with Abraham, Isaac, and Jacob in the kingdom of heaven," while in 19:28 the Twelve receive this promise: "In the new world, when the Son of man shall sit on his glorious throne, you who have followed me will also sit on twelve thrones, judging the twelve tribes of Israel." The following chapter records the dispute among the Twelve as to who will receive the thrones in the places of honor —on either side of Jesus in His kingdom.

The strongest evidence for the kingdom yet to come still remains, however. We refer to the apocalyptic discourse of chapter 24. Jesus sets out a series of indications in answer to His disciples' query: "What will be the sign of your coming and of the close of the age?" (24:3). He reveals that the end will be accompanied by cataclysmic upheavals of nature and celestial phenomena. It will be heralded by social disintegration, strife and bloodshed, and religious deceptions. But, while Jesus gives *signs* of the end, no man knows its precise date—"not even the angels of heaven, nor the Son, but the Father only" (24:36).

Thus the Christian must remain continually ready. The end, although indicated by the collapse of the natural and social worlds, will catch men unawares, just as did the great Flood. The keynote then must be: "Watch therefore, for you do not know on what day your Lord is coming." "Therefore you also must be ready; for the Son of man is coming at an hour you do not expect" (24:42, 44).

some scholars are not comfortable with a Jesus who believes in the end of the world!

Yes, God's reign broke in upon human existence with the coming of Jesus Christ. It invested the human lot with a meaning that the passing of the ages cannot dim. In that simple life of gentle and noble deeds, and above all in its strange ending—an execution on a Roman cross—divine power was manifest. God has come close to man in a unique manner, even as the Babe of Bethlehem was the Immanuel sign—"God with us" (1:23).

But that life of grace did not exhaust the rule of God. Just as the kingdom did not come to an end with the tragedy of Calvary, so it was not fully comprehended by the Incarnation. The "already" of the gentle life of Jesus is balanced by the "not yet" of the future, glorious reign.

Regarding Time and Us

It seems to me that the subject matter of this chapter speaks to men today with unusual force in three particular aspects.

First, there is the matter of the *meaning* of existence. Twentieth-century man is adrift in a sea of desperation.

"We look before and after,
  And pine for what is not:
  Our sincerest laughter
  With some pain is fraught;
  Our sweetest songs are
  Those that tell of saddest thought"[7]

was the echo of an earlier age. But T. S. Eliot captured ours:

"Here we go round the prickly pear
  Prickly pear, prickly pear
  Here we go round the prickly pear
  At five o'clock in the morning."[8]

Many of the greatest writers of our century, such as Camus, Heidegger, and Sartre, have portrayed the essentially meaningless character of life on our planet.

---

[7] Shelley, "To a Skylark."

[8] In "The Hollow Men."

Matthew's Gospel provides a radical alternative. It sees in an event in time, a *real* event—not a legend, not a fantasy, not a dream, not a hope—that which stamps history decisively for all time. Nothing, it tells us, can add to the place of Calvary. Nothing can diminish its force. That is why every loaf of bread we buy bears an imprint of an invisible cross, why every glass of water likewise is marked by a cross.[9] Calvary is the watershed of history, and thereby it makes life—*our* life—meaningful today.

Second, there is the matter of grim *forebodings* as we approach the close of the second millennium. All around we can hear prophets of doom. Today we find a remarkable parallel with the late 900's. The dawn of the new millennium is the precursor of the end of the world. But now there is a radical difference. The prophets of doom are not churchmen or wild-eyed fanatics but sober scientists, sociologists, and statesmen. The good planet Earth reels from crisis upon crisis—too many people, too little food; polluted air, polluted waters; arms race, rising crime; collapse of democratic institutions, failure of leadership; energy shortages, economic woes; climatic changes, age of famines.

[9] Note this beautiful comment (drawn from the Communion Service): "To the death of Christ we owe even this earthly life. The bread we eat is the purchase of His broken body. The water we drink is bought by His spilled blood. Never one, saint or sinner, eats his daily food, but he is nourished by the body and the blood of Christ. The cross of Calvary is stamped on every loaf. It is reflected in every water spring" (*The Desire of Ages*, p. 660).

Surely there is much to be grim about. The news is always bad. But Matthew's Gospel would encourage us. It would remind us, first of all, of the reign of God which the coming of Jesus Christ inaugurated. We are not to think of this world as abandoned to the blind forces of chance. Our world is a *special* place. It is the arena of God's mighty acts, of the supreme manifestation in the life and teachings of Jesus Christ. With Him, the kingdom came. God is with us.

Hence, the Christian lives on the knife-edge of time. He lives for today, leaning into the future. There is the joy of the "already"—and it is great! "Why," said Jesus, "your Father cares for the sparrows, even the lilies of the field. Will He not much more care for you? Why take anxious thought about tomorrow? Tomorrow will look after itself." And there is the hope of the "not yet." The joy he now finds is but the tinkle of a bell that awaits the trumpet blast of God's tomorrow. In the fullness of time the Lord of history will usher in the kingdom in the plenitude of glory.

Finally there is the matter of *Christian confidence*. While scientists proclaim the imminent end, many Christians act as if heaven were already realized. They exhibit a strange self-confidence in the name of the Holy Spirit and charismatic acts. Their enthusiasm would collapse faith into presumption.

Such misunderstandings of the Christian life are not new. Already in the days of Paul, the apostle had to correct the boasting of the Corinthians who acted as though the kingdom had come in its fullness. Matthew likewise safeguards against such distortions of the kingdom. While we *do* have the blessings of the "already" of God's kingdom, the end is not yet, he would warn us. Christian confidence is good and necessary—so long as it is not misguided. It needs to be a confidence that is *grounded in history* (not on a flight of feeling), which *rests on the achievement of Calvary* (not on an ecstatic utterance or charismatic deed), and which *looks expectantly to the full coming in of the kingdom in glory*. In a word, Christian confidence, in this time of the "not yet," must ever be muted. The joy of fulfillment always rests in the cradle of anticipation.

We are now ready to consider a final theme in Matthew's Gospel —the cross.

Chapter 7

The Cross—
His and Mine

So we come at last to the cross, as always we must. Here all other motifs from Jesus' life find their *raison d'etre*. Here the religion of Jesus reaches its crown. Here theology must both begin and end.

The cross holds a strange power of attraction. It shocks us, it amazes us, but it draws us inexorably. Men of all faiths feel its magnetism. I have seen pictures of the *crucified* Jesus hanging on the walls of Hindu temples—along with Rama, Krishna, and Lakshmi. Nor does its power wane with the passing of the years. Even in a technological age when man leaves his footprints in moondust, the cross is a ubiquitous symbol.[1]

It is exceedingly difficult for us to grasp what the cross of Jesus was really like. We look back on that Good Friday through a golden haze of a world ennobled by His cross. At the very least, Jesus' cross stands for a gross miscarriage of justice, a tragic end to a gentle and beautiful Life. With all the despisers of Christianity, one is hard put to find a man who will affirm that Jesus of Nazareth was a bad man and that Golgotha was His rightful desert. But to countless thousands in all lands of earth, the cross is far more than a blot on the record of human societies. The cross to them affords a source of peace and healing, light and life. It is the moment par excellence in Jesus' ministry, the instrument of their deliverance from sin.

Hence we erect crosses to enshrine the memory of the noble dead. Crosses are the badges of Christian edifices. Bishops—and individual Christians—parade their religiosity by a cross hung from the neck.

---

[1] Compare John 12:32: "And I, when I am lifted up from the earth, will draw all men to myself."

The Romans were not the first to erect crosses. To the Phoenicians must belong the credit for this dubious invention of execution.[2] But the Romans certainly employed the cross as a fearful deterrent against rebellion. They erected thousands of crosses around the empire—public warnings to any who might contemplate revolt. We note: *public* warnings. The process of execution by the cross must be enhanced for maximum effect. So they paraded the victim to the place of execution—bearing his cross, or the crossbar of it. As he trudged through the streets all could see a man marked for excruciating death, and well might they shiver. The cross itself was erected in a public place: Let the crowds come out to see the sights on their evening walks. (To what grisly factor in the human psyche does a public dying so strongly appeal?) There the would-be opposer of Rome would hang—usually for days, until death from the effects of exposure, loss of body fluids, and pain brought a merciful release.

So potent is the cross symbol in our world view that it takes a supreme effort to appreciate what the cross of Jesus meant *to Him*. We forget that *His* taking of the cross radically changed its meaning. We forget that He *made* it a place of light, but it was a horror of darkness for Him. We forget that He *transformed* it into a glorious object from one of humiliation and shame. We forget that He *breathed* life into it, but for Him it stood for the ebbing away of breath and hope in a despairing death.

[2] The Phoenicians and Persians used the cross before the Romans. For a compact treatment of crucifixion, see the articles by Pierson Parker on "Cross" and "Crucifixion" in *The Interpreter's Dictionary of the Bible*.

The Roman cross, in its public display and warning, epitomized *shame and humiliation*. The condemned man, after carrying his own cross, was stripped. Then he was either nailed or tied to the cross. His movements restricted, he was at the mercy of ants and other insects that would crawl over him. He could not care for his bodily needs. And the crowd on their evening stroll would taunt and deride.

No wonder that citizens of the empire were not crucified. No matter how great a Roman's crime, he was not to be subjected to the public ignominy of the cross. When on rare occasions citizens were crucified—as by Verres in Sicily and by Galla in Spain—the Romans reacted with fury against their leaders.

But Roman citizenship was hard to come by in the first century AD. Jesus of Nazareth was not a citizen; so He could be crucified.[3] And He was—on a *Roman* cross (let us never forget it: a *Roman* cross, not a Christian cross).

We shall turn to consider Matthew's account of the cross. It is not our intent to tread again the Via Dolorosa, to recount the details of Jesus' last hours. That great story has been told over and over—and let it ever be! Our concern, however, is to see the *distinctively* Matthean aspects as he recounts Jesus' Passion. But we must go further. Jesus spoke of the cross, in two contexts—His own and His disciples'. What, then, will be *my* cross, and how will it relate to the cross of Jesus Himself? Thus, we will be led to see the significance of the cross for the life of the church in these days.

I. Jesus' Cross: the Matthean Passion Story

As with the accounts of Jesus' birth, we are used to combining the various records of the Crucifixion. It comes as something of a shock to look at Matthew's description in isolation from the composite picture.

---

[3] But Paul was a citizen (see Acts 16:37; 22:26-29; 23:27). So he met his death by the sword, not by crucifixion (see *The Acts of the Apostles,* p. 511: "the sword of the executioner").

If we take Matthew 27:27-50 on its own, one stark fact impresses us: *the desolation of Jesus*. Absent are the "words" from the cross: "Father, forgive them; for they know not what they do. . . . You will be with me in Paradise. . . . Woman, behold your son! . . . [Son], behold your mother! . . . I thirst. . . . It is finished. . . . Into thy hands I commend my spirit." Instead, Matthew records but one saying of Jesus, the agonized, "My God, my God, why hast thou forsaken me?" (27:46).

Only here do we find Matthew referring to Jesus' actual speech. The Gospels, like all the New Testament, are written in Greek, but Jesus spoke the language of the people of His day—Aramaic. In three places Mark's Gospel preserves Jesus' actual Aramaic sayings: in the "Talitha cumi ["Little girl, . . . arise"]" (5:41) addressed to Jairus' daughter; in the "Ephphatha ["Be opened"]" (7:34) spoken to the deaf, speech-impaired man; and from the cross in the "Eloi, Eloi, lama sabachthani? ["My God, My God, why have You forsaken Me?"]" (15:34). Matthew passes over the first two instances but preserves the Aramaic saying from the cross. Indeed, as we noticed above, this is the *only* saying of Jesus on the cross which he records.

Why does Matthew revert to the actual speech of Jesus at this one point? Assuredly because the saying is so stark, so filled with woe, that many Christians were having difficulty in accepting its genuineness.

The saying, in fact, epitomizes the Matthean Crucifixion scene. The picture we have of Jesus on the cross is unrelieved in its gloom. There is no loving disciple nearby, no repentant thief, no cry of triumph at the close. Instead, we see mocking, rejection, derision, reviling, darkness—and at last a loud cry in the final moment of death.

It is true that Matthew's story of the cross closely parallels Mark's. Matthew, however, highlights Jesus' utter desolation because of the manner in which he has described the events immediately prior to Good Friday. If we compare Matthew 26:14, 36, with Mark 14:12, 32, we note the heightening of dramatic effect in Matthew's account: (1) Matthew uses "then" (Greek: *tote*) where Mark uses merely "and" (*kai*); and (2) reports given in Mark 14:23, 32-39 are transformed into direct speech in Matthew 26:27, 36, 38-40, 42. The effect is to make the Jesus of the Last Supper scenes more *majestic* in Matthew's Gospel. Indeed, Matthew commences chapter 26 with these words: "When Jesus had finished all these sayings, he said to his disciples, 'You know that after two days the Passover is coming, and the Son of man will be delivered up to be crucified.' *Then* the chief priests and the elders of the people gathered." Here is a Jesus who is in command, who speaks the word, and it is done. Note His instructions with regard to preparations for the Last Supper. Because He has spoken, it is assumed to be as He has described (Matthew 26:17-19; see also Mark 14:12-16): They "found it as he had told them."

The Messiah, in command, majestic in bearing, then the utter desolation of the cross scene! Truly the forlorn words, "My God, my God . . ." stand as the signature of Jesus' cross.

While the actual Crucifixion in Matthew's Gospel is set out in these stark terms, we should notice also three distinctive features of his Passion account. He alone records the dream of Pilate's wife, Pilate's washing of his hands, and the resurrection of the saints. We shall look briefly at each of these unique aspects.

As Pilate sits on the judgment seat, endeavoring to have Jesus released, a word comes from his wife. " 'Have nothing to do with that righteous man,' " she says, " 'for I have suffered much over him today in a dream' " (27:19). So the end resembles the beginning: As Jesus in His birth and infancy was the object of dreams, so in His final moments. Matthew heightens the numinous element. Here is no ordinary prisoner, not even an innocent rabbi! No, He is One whose being is linked to the supernatural world. This feature further sharpens the drama that has built up through the previous scenes—and correspondingly renders the darkness of the Crucifixion, soon to follow, even more dense.

But Pilate cannot release Jesus —the crowd wants Him crucified. "So when Pilate saw that he was gaining nothing, but rather that a riot was beginning, he took water and washed his hands before the crowd, saying, 'I am innocent of this man's blood; see to it yourselves.' And all the people answered, 'His blood be on us and on our children!' " (27:24, 25).

Matthew lays the guilt of Jesus' death squarely on the Jews. Pilate washes his hands and declares, " 'I am innocent,' " and the fearful responsibility is admitted, yes, even claimed, " 'His blood be on us and on our children!' " Whether or not Matthew wants us to absolve Pilate is not the point here. Clearly he is concerned in showing the tragedy of the rejection of Jesus *by His own people*. The inscription on His cross now rings with a bitter tone: "This is Jesus the King of the Jews." For Matthew, we recall, has all along shown that Jesus is in fact Israel's King. He is the One of the royal line, He to whom the Old Testament bore witness, the long-awaited Messiah. Now He has come, and His own people have cried out for His blood. Cried out—and got it! "He came to his own home, and his own people received him not" (John 1:11).

The third Matthean feature is the most notable of all. Just as soon as we have read the infinitely sad account of the cross and Jesus' final cry, Matthew relates: "And behold, the curtain of the temple was torn in two, from top to bottom; and the earth shook, and the rocks were split; the tombs also were opened, and many bodies of the saints who had fallen asleep were raised, and coming out of the tombs after his resurrection they went into the holy city and appeared to many" (27:51-53).

The contrast could hardly be more striking. The resurrection of the dead was expected as one of the events of the end, the demonstration that Messiah had come at last.[4] Now, just after the death scene, the earth is rent, preparing for the resurrection of some of the righteous on Easter Sunday. Thus he immediately prepares us for a new evaluation of Jesus' sad demise, an evaluation summed up in the words of the centurion which follow at once, " 'Truly this was the Son of God!' " and confirmed by the glorious evidence of chapter 28.

---

[4] This is the basis of the reasoning in Paul's great chapter on the Resurrection, 1 Corinthians 15. Instead of arguing that if Christ is not raised there is no resurrection of the dead, he says, "But if there is no resurrection of the dead, then Christ has not been raised" (verse 13).

Thus the three distinctively Matthean features together serve to heighten the pathos of the actual cross of Jesus. The first two, which are precross, point in turn to the special character of the One who is to be put on the cross and the tragedy of His rejection by those who claimed to look for His arrival. The third, which is postcross, dramatically reinforces the precross view of Jesus as Messiah, Israel's King—a view that has been cast upon the winds of confusion by the desolation of the Crucifixion scene. For there stands the cross, *His* cross—stark, remote, naked, horrible. It stands in darkness. It stands in desolation. Around it swirl the taunts and the jeers. And from it issues a piteous lament: "My God, My God, why have *You* forsaken Me?"[5]

II. My Cross

Many thousands of crosses were erected over the centuries. But one was unique—Jesus' cross. Perhaps after that the cross could never be the same again. Perhaps it is not at all surprising that the cross gradually dropped out of use as a means of execution, for after *His* cross it began to symbolize a new religion and a new way of life. The old "torture stick" could *never* be the same again.

So when we speak of the Christian's cross, we cannot begin to put it on a level with His. His has a historic significance, once-for-all quality, and (let us not forget it!) a *concrete reality* before which all talk about our crosses fades into a whisper.

[5] We are not to hide the *desolation* of the cross. Note especially the emphasis on this aspect of the cross in *The Desire of Ages,* pp. 751, 753, 754, 756. So we are counseled not to cover the cross with ornamental roses (Ellen G. White, *Sons and Daughters of God,* p. 266). The cross was "ignominious" (*Testimonies to Ministers,* p. 67).

Nevertheless Matthew's Gospel does refer in two places to the Christian's cross. The first occurrence is in the great mission chapter. As Jesus has described the hardships that those who would follow Him are to expect, we find this word: "And he who does not take his cross and follow me is not worthy of me" (10:38). The second passage comes after the rebuke to Peter at Caesarea Philippi: "Then Jesus told his disciples, 'If any man would come after me, let him deny himself and take up his cross and follow me'" (16:24).

What do these words mean? They mean a sense in which each Christian is *individually* called upon to participate in some measure in the Master's experience. In both verses the accent falls on *he, any man.* Just as Jesus endured the cross alone, so the Christian's cross can be shared by no other. We meet our Lord in a one-to-one relationship which brings with it a cross. The Christian's cross is always individualized. Better, it is personalized, hence *my* cross.

Here is the counterpart of the corporate aspect of Christianity which we denote by "the church." The church is a fellowship, a community, and a communion of those who have heard the call of the Man from Galilee. We must never devalue it, never dismiss it lightly—even if many in our age would do so. But Christianity in the final analysis begins with an *individual's* response to Jesus Christ, who claims lordship over the life. It calls for a personal decision that father or mother, sister or brother, husband or wife, cannot make for the other. There is no cross-bearing by proxy. The words immediately preceding the cross statement in chapter 10 underscore this point: No man is worthy of Jesus who cares more for father or mother, son or daughter.

But what *precisely* is entailed by the Christian's cross—*my* cross? Is it a hardship, an individual handicap that each Christian may have thrust upon him? Is it (as some would maintain) a nagging wife, an errant digestive tract, or an irascible employer?

No, the Christian's cross is none of these. As we look closely at the content of the cross sayings, two features come clearly into view—*shame* and *death*.

The cross as a symbol of shame is sharply indicated in chapter 10. Jesus has spoken about acknowledging (or denying) Him before men (verses 32, 33). Then He turns to the divisive character of the new religion: A man will find his enemies under his own roof (verses 34-36). After the saying stressing the individuality of decision which He calls forth (verse 37), the cross saying appears.

It is hard for us to appreciate the *shame* of the cross. Only as we put ourselves back in the first century —in that precross era—can we catch the obloquy and scorn which crucifixion evoked. Only as we meditate on Paul's "word of the cross" (1 Corinthians 1:18-25)— foolishness to the Greeks, a scandal to the Jews—can we begin to grasp the shame of being associated with the One whose signature was and is the cross.

In distant lands where the message of Jesus does not hold sway, one may yet catch something of the original import of the cross sayings. It is devastating for the Muslim or the Hindu to become a Christian. It involves far more than a change of religion. The convert finds himself cut off from family, community, caste, and employment. The social and psychological pressures are intense. The cross as a symbol of shame is a poignant reality.

But *my* cross goes beyond this aspect. Indeed, there is little shame in declaring oneself a Christian in the United States—though I suspect that he who would truly follow Jesus will not infrequently have to stand on his own, as it were, and be considered "soft in the head" by associates. The second and more urgently vital aspect of *my* cross is that of *death*. The contents of both sayings point unerringly in this direction. In each case the discussion immediately following the talk of the cross speaks of losing one's life for Jesus' sake, or seeking to hold it—and so losing it eternally.

My cross—death? The thought is frightening. We would much prefer to put up with an obstinate spouse or a rheumatic back! But we must remind ourselves of the original setting of the words, of that first-century milieu in which they are rooted. In that age, beyond question the cross symbolized death.

You see a line of men, dragging down the road. What are they bearing on their shoulders? And why are those soldiers with them? Ah, the crosses! Poor wretches, they are on their way to a ghastly execution.

Now here is another. He, too, bears a cross. See, He stoops, stumbles, falls beneath its weight. How pale He looks! Who is He? Can He be the itinerant teacher from the north, the preacher-healer who has set Jerusalem abuzz with expectation? Yes, it is He, Jesus from Nazareth! So they have got Him at last, have they? They are going to put Him out of the way, to *crucify* Him!

Look, He is speaking! What are those words that fall from His bloodstained lips? "No man is worthy of me who does not take up his cross and walk in my footsteps. . . . If any man wishes to be a follower of mine, he must leave self behind; he must take up his cross and come with me."

"Jesus, I my cross have taken,
All to leave and follow Thee;
All things else I have forsaken;
Thou from hence my all shall be."

My cross signifies *acceptance* of Jesus, the Crucified One. It signifies *identification* with Him. It signifies *participation* with Him by way of that cross.

My cross still stands for death. That is why we shrink from it, seek to substitute for it. The death is not a martyr's stake in these days, but it is just as real—the death of self. By taking up *my* cross I renounce my grasping ego, I renounce my attempts at acting out the God-role, I renounce *my* self which wants to play it safe for itself. I renounce *all* so that I might receive *all* in a new person-hood as a follower of Jesus Christ.

III. The Cross and the Church

Crosses are in fashion. Think of all the steeples, all the stained-glass windows, all the altars, all the pendant crosses. No doubt the manufacture of crosses benefits the economy.

Perhaps, however, we need to hear again the "word of the cross." Perhaps it is *the church* that needs most to hear it. Could it be that the parading of our religiosity by actual physical symbols in fact parades our need of hearing that word? Could it be that the language of our piety—our sentimental songs about Jesus' sufferings, even our tears at His wounds, are a mask to hide our paganism?

Lest we reject these words as too harsh (for harsh they are), let us remind ourselves of a few lessons from history. The physical symbol of the cross cannot guarantee the genuineness of our religion. Was it not the banner under which "Christians" slaughtered "the infidels" in bygone times? Neither does preoccupation with Jesus' sufferings prove our Christianity. We may retreat into the cloister to contemplate His pain while the world of which He was part and which He came to redeem plunges headlong into ruin.

No, the cross speaks this word to the church: It is a way of life in the world. It is a way of life which has as its badge the Crucified One.[6]

The cross stands for reversal. One's scale of judging oneself and others is reversed. One's view of the world is turned about. That which the world despises is now most precious, and that which it holds dear is seen as a thing of naught. He whom the world rejects —crucifies—is now the Lord, and as for Barabbas, let him free to those who want him!

The church must never forget that the cross is still the signature of Jesus. It must never become so fascinated with business techniques and the love of mammon that it subtly changes sides. Let the awful fact of history ever confront it: The *religious leaders* of the day were those who led out in the death of Jesus. Could it, even while minting its crosses and singing songs of Calvary, become so duped by the deceitful power of evil that all unwittingly it has joined forces with the mob?[7]

But, after all, who is the church? *We* are the church. *I* am the church. So the cross at last addresses me in my life as a Christian. It calls for more than a once-for-all decision to accept Jesus as my Saviour from sin. That is important, very important, but as a Christian, the cross calls me to a particular *way of life* in the world. The cross brings with it a cross-ethic.

I am not persuaded that the world has been converted. I am not convinced that the West is Christian. The cross still comes as a reproach and a stumbling block. The way of the cross is a way of weakness, a way of submission, a way devoid of cunning, artfulness, and sleight of hand. He who takes the cross as his signature must be counted a fool.[8]

A fool—unless his whole world view has been reversed by that cross! Then he sees that the way of weakness, the way of submission, the way of transparent honesty is the *right* way, the *divine* way. And why? Because it is the way of love.

In a sinful world love will always carry a cross.

[6] "But the cross does not become just the way to lordship or the price paid for it. Rather, it remains the signature of the risen Lord. He possesses no other visage except the countenance of the Crucified, and only under this countenance can we take our stand" (Ernst Käsemann, "The Pauline Theology of the Cross," *Interpretation,* April, 1970, p. 174).

[7] Instead, let Ellen White's words be the experience of the church: "We behold in the cross of Christ our efficiency, our inexhaustible source of power" (Letter 129, 1898). Again, "If those who today are teaching the word of God, would uplift the cross of Christ higher and still higher, their ministry would be far more successful. If sinners can be led to give one earnest look at the cross, if they can obtain a full view of the crucified Saviour, they will realize the depth of God's compassion

So we conclude our study of the major themes of Matthew's Gospel. We have, in the past six chapters, looked at the Jesus of this Gospel and at its great ideas—discipleship, righteousness, the church, the kingdom, and the cross. As we draw our final conclusions in the next chapter, we shall be concerned with the *occasion* for Matthew's document—why and to whom he wrote it.

and the sinfulness of sin" (*The Acts of the Apostles,* p. 209. See the whole chapter from which this selection is taken, "Exalting the Cross").

[8] That the cross stood for a way of life in the world is abundantly clear in the Pauline writings. Paul's view of the gospel, of Jesus, and of his own apostleship is to be comprehended under one term—the cross (see Philippians 2:1-11; 1 Corinthians 2:1-4; 2 Corinthians 13:4, 5; Galatians 6:14; Philippians 3:4-11; 2 Corinthians 11:4-6, 30; 12:5, 10-13).

Chapter 8

Retrospect— Religion in Overalls

The Book of Matthew did not drop down whole from the heavens. Its words were not dictated by a divine Spirit to a human agent. It arose out of a particular historical setting and is therefore a creation in time and space.[1] While we affirm that there is an extra *something*, an added factor which sets this writing apart from others —the word of man is also the word of God—we must take account of the historical context. The more we can unravel of the situation which called forth Matthew's Gospel, the better we may grasp its message.

Scholars have long recognized that Matthew's Gospel is set against the backdrop of a debate with Judaism. Christianity was cradled in Judaism, and the original apostles and first believers were all Jews. Only slowly did the concept of the followers of Jesus expand to worldwide dimension, which came as they saw that the religion of Jesus was, in fact, a *new* religion. It was new wine which old wineskins could not long contain (Mark 2:22). The rupture with the old tradition was inevitable—but nonetheless painful for all.

---

[1] Note especially the following statement from Ellen G. White:

"There is variety in a tree, there are scarcely two leaves just alike. Yet this variety adds to the perfection of the tree as a whole.

"In our Bible, we might ask, Why need Matthew, Mark, Luke, and John in the Gospels, why need the Acts of the Apostles, and the variety of writers in the Epistles, go over the same thing?

"The Lord gave His word in just the way He wanted it to come. He gave it through different writers, each having his own individuality, though going over the same history. Their testimonies are brought together in one Book, and are like the testimonies in a social meeting. They do not represent things in just the same style. Each has an experience of his own, and this diversity broadens and deepens the knowledge that is brought out to meet the

It is not possible for us to pinpoint the date for the parting of the ways. The Book of Acts, with its programmatic account of the mission of the followers of Jesus—first in Jerusalem, then in Judea and Samaria, then to the uttermost parts of the earth (Acts 1:8)—gives a broad outline of the evolution of Christianity as a new, separate, universal religion. Certainly the year AD 70 is a significant one. In that year the armies of Rome under Titus captured Jerusalem and put the Temple to the torch. It was a severe blow to Judaism as well as to the pro-Jewish wing of Christianity. Jerusalem, the mother church, lost its position of preeminence and suffered a steady decline until AD 135, when Jerusalem was again destroyed by the Romans and all Jews were expelled. There was a corresponding cleavage from Christianity on the part of Judaism itself. The Jewish Christians had dissociated themselves from the struggle with Rome. Now Judaism wanted no truck with them. There could no longer be any question of looking upon the followers of Jesus of Nazareth as a sect within the Jewish fold. Indeed, in the period immediately following the fall of Jerusalem, as the leaders of Judaism sought to regroup to save their religion, they took a measure which effectively banned Christians from the synagogue services. In the prayers for public worship they inserted a curse upon the followers of Jesus.[2]

necessities of varied minds. The thoughts expressed have not a set uniformity, as if cast in an iron mold, making the very hearing monotonous. In such uniformity there would be a loss of grace and distinctive beauty. . . .

"The Creator of all ideas may impress different minds with the same thought, but each may express it in a different way, yet without contradiction. The fact that this difference exists should not perplex or confuse us. It is seldom that two persons will view and express truth in the very same way. Each dwells on particular points which his constitution and education have fitted him to appreciate. The sunlight falling upon the different objects gives those objects a different hue.

"Through the inspiration of His Spirit the Lord gave His apostles truth, to be expressed according to the development of their minds by the Holy Spirit. But the

Matthew's Gospel reflects this situation of tension with Judaism. The Christians whom he addresses obviously have strong ties with the ancient religion. Perhaps the final parting of the ways has not yet been reached—but it is near. The Messiah has appeared. The predictions of the Old Testament have met their fulfillment. The King has come. The rule of God has been inaugurated. But Judaism has failed to recognize her King, who is lowly and crowned with thorns, and she has refused to acknowledge that the divine kingdom has already broken through. The new wine must soon burst from the old wineskins.

The situation pictured in the above remarks has frequently been commented upon.[3] It seems to me, however, that there is more to be said than this. As we have studied the great themes of Matthew's Gospel in the previous chapters, the reader may have noticed a factor obtruding itself over and over again—charismatic Christianity. It seems to me that a good case can be made out for his Gospel's being written as a response to the claims of an early Christian "enthusiasmus."[4] Let us look at this thesis more closely.

mind is not cramped, as if forced into a certain mold" (Selected Messages, Book One, pp. 21, 22).

[2] This curse was inserted in the Eighteen Benedictions (these benedictions are still in use, but the curse has since been modified). Thus Judaism ensured that the follower of Jesus Christ would be forced to dissociate himself from the worship service of the synagogue.

[3] G. D. Kilpatrick in The Origins of the Gospel According to St. Matthew, pp. 101-123, for instance, suggests that the Jewish opposition in Matthew's Gospel accords with the situation which Christianity faced in the period AD 70 to 135.

[4] The German enthusiasmus is not quite equivalent to our English enthusiasm. It suggests a heightened emphasis on personal religious experience and the possession of

Matthew and the Charismatics

The first matter which we should notice is Matthew's reference to the Spirit. A quick comparison with the other Gospels puts us on the track. Whereas Luke has six references to the Holy Spirit and John has twelve, Matthew has only five.[5] Of these, four are applied to Jesus Himself (3:16; 4:1; 12:18, 28). The sole reference which associates the Spirit with the disciples is at 10:20: "It is not you who speak, but the Spirit of your Father speaking through you."

The *significance* of these data becomes clear when we study closely the references to "Spirit." *Matthew seems deliberately to avoid linking discipleship with Spirit possession.*

Matthew 7 provides a striking illustration. Whereas the Lucan parallel reads, "If you then, who are evil, know how to give good gifts to your children, how much more will the heavenly Father give the Holy Spirit to those who ask him!" (Luke 11:13), Matthew leaves out any reference to the Spirit, instead having the generalized "good gifts": "If you then, who are evil, know how to give good gifts to your children, how much more will your Father who is in heaven give good things to those who ask him!" (7:11).

The various conclusions of the Gospel narratives make the same point. Just as the commencement of each Gospel lays the backdrop for the portrayal of Jesus which will follow, so the conclusion of each provides the finale appropriate to that portrayal and also serves as a window into the author's conception of the church. Here the Gospels of Luke and John show the strongest dissimilarities from Matthew's.

---

the Spirit. The idea goes back to the Greek notion of the mantic reveler who is *en theos* (literally, "in God").

[5] Mark has only two references to the Holy Spirit; however, in the long ending of his Gospel a strong passage advocates charismatic Christianity (16:17, 18).

In Luke the ministry of Jesus is a ministry par excellence of the Spirit. Luke's companion volume, the Acts, sums up well the conception of the life and work of Jesus: "God anointed Jesus of Nazareth with the Holy Spirit and with power; ... he went about doing good and healing all that were oppressed by the devil, for God was with him" (Acts 10:38). It was a ministry already intimated in the sermon at Nazareth which Luke chooses as the introduction to Jesus' public life: "The Spirit of the Lord is upon me" (Luke 4:18).

Accordingly, the Gospel concludes with Jesus' admonition to wait for the heavenly empowering. What that empowering means is explained in Acts 1:8: "You shall be anointed with the Holy Ghost"—a promise which finds fulfillment in Acts 2. Then throughout the rest of the book the Spirit empowers the disciples, guides the church, and brings conviction to the apostolic preaching. Thus the deeds of the disciples recapitulate the deeds of their Master recorded in the Gospel of Luke.

The fourth Gospel goes even further. While John does not stress the personal presence of the Spirit in the life and deeds of Jesus (probably because the deity of the Son is underlined from the opening words), Jesus, in chapter 7, verse 37, is set forth as He who will send the Spirit on His disciples after the Crucifixion. "If any one thirst, let him come to me and drink," He cries out at the Feast of Tabernacles. The evangelist explains that the meaning is to be found in the gift of the Spirit which was not yet given (verse 39). The famous farewell discourse (chapters 14-16) is replete with this idea. Jesus is going away, but His followers are not to be left orphans. He will send the Paraclete, the divine Advocate, or Comforter, who will remain with them forever. He will lead them into all truth, recall the words of Jesus to their memory, glorify Jesus, and convict the world of sin, righteousness, and judgment. Accordingly, in John 20:22 we find the risen Christ breathing upon His disciples the words: "Receive the Holy Spirit."

Mark is not like Luke and John in emphasizing the Spirit, but he is far closer to them than to Matthew. The first picture of Jesus' ministry—an exorcism—establishes the pattern. He portrays Jesus as a mighty miracle worker, one whose deeds leave people gasping in wonder. Some manuscripts of Mark's Gospel close it with such a scene (there is confusion in the ancient Greek texts as to where Mark originally ended). They abruptly end at 16:8, with the women followers of Jesus speechless at Jesus' supreme act—the empty tomb. The longer ending of Mark, however—the one with which readers of the King James Version are familiar—gives a very different picture. Chapter 16, verses 17 and 18, shows the risen Christ conferring upon His followers all manner of miraculous powers: "And these signs will accompany those who believe: in my name they will cast out demons; they will speak in new tongues; they will pick up serpents, and if they drink any deadly thing, it will not hurt them; they will lay their hands on the sick, and they will recover." Although Mark does not mention the Spirit here, the passage is the quintessence of charismatic Christianity. Here the snake-handling cults in the mountains of east Tennessee find their *raison d'etre*.

Matthew stands strangely alone in this company. He is clearly the odd man out. The risen Christ says not a word about the Spirit—only that in the Threefold Name the disciples from all the world are to be baptized. Just as the ministry contained no promise of a Spirit to be confirmed after the death, so the Resurrected One does not act to bring down the Spirit on His followers. Nor does He empower them with fantastic powers over serpents, poisons, and disease.

But does not Jesus work miracles? Is He not a charismatic figure even in Matthew's Gospel? While we must answer both questions in the affirmative, we have to add this: the miracles and the charismatic Jesus are subordinated to the concept of the King of humility. "Not with swords, loud clashing, nor roll of stirring drums," not with dazzling deeds that stupefy the crowds, does the kingdom of Jesus break through to man. But, "Blessed are the poor in spirit, for theirs is the kingdom of heaven." "Behold your king, . . . humble, and mounted on an ass" (5:3; 21:5).

Thus Matthew comes down with particular severity on those Christians who would flaunt their charismatic prowess. Not your wonders! Not your exorcisms! Not your preachings! Don't try to boast before God! Or you will be surprised—surprised out of your eternal life—in the judgment. Not your miracles—but your *deeds!* How have you *lived?* Have you kept *God's* will? Which means, What have you done about those *words* that tell you about that will?

Instead He leaves with them—His words. But those words convey to them authority and ensure that He will be with them forever, even to the close of the age. And is not this the pattern which we already have learned from Matthew's Gospel? Was not Matthew concerned with *words* from the outset of Jesus' ministry? Did he not focus that ministry in the description of its commencement—the magnificent Sermon on the Mount? Did he not structure his story of Jesus around the five great discourses? And did he not also downplay the part of the Spirit in the ministry, giving only two references, and one of these in a quotation whose thrust is to emphasize the unobtrusiveness of the work of Jesus rather than the Spirit per se?[6]

---

[6] This is in 12:18, where Isaiah 42:1-4 is quoted and applied to Jesus. The context (10:15-17) clearly shows that the ministry of Jesus was deliberately concerned to avoid public display. (The other reference to the Spirit in Jesus' ministry is at 12:28, which we have already noticed in chapter 6. The Spirit here is a sign of the break-in of the kingdom of God.)

Can it be by chance that Matthew obviously has turned from *enthusiasmus*—a Christianity of the Spirit and charismatic acts? Surely he was not ignorant of the Spirit's place in the early church. We would like to roll back the curtains to look into the situation addressed by Matthew. Why would he so deemphasize charismatic Christianity? Why—if he had not become aware of gross abuses in the name of the Spirit, of distortions of the gospel in the name of the charismata? Did he feel that it was time someone wrote a corrective, put a brake on *enthusiasmus?* Did he endeavor to *balance* the account, as it were, to put Jesus' life and work in perspective—and hence the concept of the church in perspective also?

We cannot give a final answer. Arguments from silence are notoriously dubious. Yet it seems that the evidence from the Gospel of Matthew points strongly in the direction indicated above. He says *just* enough about the Spirit and charismatic acts to show us that he was familiar with them and afforded them a place—but he wants to show what that place is.

Now we may be ready for a final assessment of the value of Matthew's Gospel for the church today.

Religion in Overalls

Matthew and Paul. Matthew and Luke. How very different the presentations of the good news of Jesus Christ in each! So different that one is tempted to put it this way: Matthew versus Paul, Matthew versus Luke.

But that would be false to all three. Matthew is not opposing Paul any more than he is opposing Luke. Rather, he is attempting to set forth an account of Jesus Christ and His gospel in a manner that will best meet the needs of the Christians with whom he is acquainted. Paul does the same; so does Luke. Let us never forget this great fact about the New Testament writings: Each is a product of *time* and *place,* written to meet a particular situation in the life of the church. Each has a message for its own age—and a message edged with particular sharpness for a specific group of Jesus' followers in that age.

It is pointless to inject questions of "inspiration" into the discussion. We must avoid playing off Paul against Matthew or Luke against Matthew, assigning a priority of spiritual value, or before long we will find ourselves caught up arguing for degrees of inspiration. The great Luther erred at this point. He set up a canon within the canon. Let us not fall into a similar pit.

No, let us learn a lesson from the life of the church today. One preacher may present the gospel with one emphasis and another with a different one—but it is the same gospel. The subject matter of Christianity is inexhaustible, too broad for the mind or work of any individual to contain. At the heart of our religion lies a mystery, the manifestation of God to man in Jesus Christ.[7] That mystery is to be the science and song of God's people throughout eternity. We must beware of the preacher who already has all the answers, who would set himself up as the sole repository of truth and its proclamation. Did not Paul *vary* his presentation of the gospel? Where, for instance, does one find the classical outline of the Pauline "righteousness by faith" in the bulky Corinthian correspondence? Paul writes according to the *needs* of his people.

117

[7] Compare 1 Timothy 3:16; also the argument in Colossians and Ephesians relative to "the mystery."

And is not that a prime demand of any presentation of the gospel—that it meet men and women *where they are?* A speaker much acclaimed in some circles once visited our home and said to our boy, "Break through the rock of inertia and life leaps like a geyser." Wonderful—except that it didn't make a bean of sense to our five-year-old. Even so, the gospel of Jesus Christ must come warm with the love of God, touching the hearts of people in terms they can understand. It must answer the questions *they* are asking. They aren't interested to hear solutions to problems which do not concern them.

The gospel is not to be abstracted, separated, from life. The gospel is God *meeting* men and women, youth, boys and girls—through Jesus Christ. Take away the living situation, and you have speculation, theory, philosophy—but *not* the gospel.

So the Gospel of Matthew must have jolted many Christians in the first century. Perhaps it offended some. Perhaps some questioned Matthew's basic understanding of the faith. But perhaps, too, a good many were led to search their hearts, to ponder and pray lest they find themselves among those who, for all their show of piety and mighty deeds, were to hear the dread words of the judgment, "I never knew you. Depart from me."

Certainly the early church in general recognized the value of this Gospel. It was one of the earliest documents to find a niche in the canon of the New Testament —where it was accorded pride of place.

Even so may the Gospel of Matthew prove to be of great value to Christians in this age. It comes as a striking corrective to much that is spoken, sung, and written today. It is not so much that Matthew is fundamentally *opposed* to charismatic Christianity as that he wishes to guard the church against its dangers. He calls us back to an objective criterion. He affirms that any *experience* in the name of Jesus Christ or the Spirit must be measured by that standard. No matter how thrilling the experience, no matter how amazing the charismata, they are to be judged—and discarded if found wanting—by the criterion. What is it that calls into question even Christian ecstasy? The criterion is the *words* of Jesus Christ.

Thus Matthew's Gospel is preeminently the gospel of Jesus' words. I have chosen a more down-to-earth description—Religion in Overalls. It is one, I think, that is fair to the Gospel and to the type of Christianity to which Jesus' words pointed. Over and over we have seen that this Gospel insists upon a *practical* type of Christianity, a Christianity that is *lived,* one that brings forth *fruit*. It is religion out in the hurly-burly of life. It is a religion lived by people who are being persecuted, who face the sad stroke of death, who struggle for their daily bread. When you are hungry, when you are struck, when you are afraid, when your heart is breaking—what then? Do you have a Christianity that has donned overalls?

Most of us are good at theorizing but pretty weak in practice. We would rather recite the doctrine than live the life, argue about theology than put the Sermon on the Mount to work. Matthew cuts across our complacency. He will not let us dodge the issue. He calls us all—every Christian, but especially the preacher, the Bible teacher, and the theologian—to account. And this is the question he thrusts on us as he fixes us with steely eye, "What of *your* religion —has it yet put on overalls?"

There is a *power* in that eye of his. Why, we ask, why does his demand meet us so irrevocably? Why cannot we simply dismiss it and turn to some delightful Christian diversion? Because of the note of *authority* behind those words, for they are not Matthew's but the Master's! As does no other Gospel, Matthew's centers in the sayings of Jesus. We may not like them (they make us feel quite uncomfortable, in fact), but we *know* that we cannot shove them aside if we are to continue to name the name of Jesus. However strong their rebuke, we must hear it—and heed it. We sense in our innermost being that we neglect them at our peril.

We must close our study of the first Gospel. We have tried to uncover the great themes of this ancient document and to show their timeliness. Yet we have made no more than a beginning. If we have succeeded in bringing out the significance of Jesus and His righteousness, discipleship, the church, the kingdom, and the cross in this book, let not the reader get the idea that we have exhausted the material. We have tapped a silver bell. An orchestra of meaning remains to be heard. But if the reader has caught the tinkle of that bell, if now he desires to hear more, if the clear note he has heard leads him on in the quest of Matthew, how much greater will be the contribution of the effort made here.

Sermons, parables, miracles; disciples, Pharisees, people—what a rich document it is! And above all, the Lord. There He is, foretold before conception by the angel, the object of adoration by the Magi, fleeing into Egypt, growing up in Nazareth, going to the Jordan, and then . . . that ministry: King of love, King of humility, King of service to mankind; miracle worker, He makes no claims for Himself, avoids ostentatious display and worldly glory; wisdom personified, He speaks—and speaks and speaks. For above all else, the Lord is the Great Teacher, whose words ring to the end of the age. Calvary cannot silence them, the tomb cannot hold them back, the ages as they pass by cannot diminish them.

Diminish them? No. They come with the authority of the risen Lord. The ages shall only increase their value, add to their conquests. "All authority in heaven and on earth has been given to me. Go therefore and make disciples of all nations, baptizing them in the name of the Father and of the Son and of the Holy Spirit, teaching them to observe all that I have commanded you; and lo, I am with you always, to the close of the age" (28:18-20).